Black Bible Chronicles

Black Bible Chronicles

Book One:
From Genesis to the Promised Land

P.K. McCary
Interpreter

African American Family Press™

AFRICAN AMERICAN FAMILY PRESS™
An imprint of Multi Media Communicators, Inc.
575 Madison Avenue, Suite 1006
New York, NY 10022

Black Bible Chronicles

Book One:
From Genesis to the Promised Land

African American Family Press™ is a trademark of Multi Media Communicators, Inc.

Cover by Lou Grant
Typesetter, Samuel Chapin

Library of Congress Catalog Card Number: 93-071549

ISBN 1-56977-000-X

10 9 8 7 6 5 4 3 2
First Edition

Printed in the United States of America

FOREWORD

The Language of the Streets

The *Black Bible Chronicles* comes at a time when significant and varied tensions are pulling at the very fabric of our society. From the Los Angeles riots to the economic distress plaguing our country, America is at an important crossroads.

While record numbers of Americans of all ages attend church regularly, ironically we are on the verge of losing a whole generation of young people. Drugs, crime, and the raging open warfare on the streets are creating a lost generation for whom communication is difficult, and hope and purpose seem only words. These are America's youth at risk.

In the midst of this growing crisis stands the Bible with its timeless message of hope and meaning in the face of despair. The Word of the Bible has a powerful message for our condition—simple yet compelling—a transforming message. And, while the message must remain the same, the language must be responsive to the times.

Important to our young people's understanding of the Word is the manner in which the Bible is communicated. To be truly relevant to their experience, it must be in a language familiar to their culture.

The *Black Bible Chronicles* is an attempt to put the most important message of life into the language of the streets. This is in keeping with the very origins of the Bible. The New Testament was originally written in Koine Greek, the street language of the people. Subsequently, Martin Luther and others translated the Bible into the language of the people of their day. The *Black Bible*

Chronicles stands in this tradition, bringing the Word to our younger generation in contemporary language.

This book seeks to reach many of our young people for whom the traditional language of faith has lost the power to bring them in touch with their God. The *Black Bible Chronicles* attempts to express a faith which addresses the deepest longings of our younger generation for hope, love, and an encouraging vision of the future.

The Honorable Andrew Young
Former Ambassador to the United Nations
Former Congressman and Mayor of Atlanta

CONTENTS

Black Bible Chronicles

The First Book of Moses

called

Genesis

And God stepped out on space,
And He looked around and said,
"I'm real lonely
I'll make me a world."

The Creation
James Weldon Johnson

World Up!

Now when the Almighty was first down with His program, He made the heavens and the earth. The earth was a fashion misfit, being so uncool and dark, but the Spirit of the Almighty came down real tough, so that He simply said, "Lighten up!" And that light was right on time. And the Almighty liked what He saw and let the light hang out a while before it was dark again. He laid out a name for the light, calling it "day" time and the dark He called "night" time so that all around it made up the first day.[1]

The Almighty's program continued, making those dark ugly masses separate so that they made up the skies above and the big waters, oceans, below. And all was happenin' (the sky above, you see, and the oceans below), creating day two.

The Almighty hung tough with His program and commanded that the waters "Get to one place," and there was land and this He called earth. The water left, He called "seas."

And He was happy.

Then He commanded the earth to be down with every kind of grass, fruit- and plant-producing tree which was like itself, and the earth was down enough to make the Almighty smile. Count 'em up, now—day three. So, the Almighty's program continued with bright lights which lit up the world at His command. The day differed from

---

[1]See Genesis, Chapter 1 for more information on the Almighty's program.

night 'round the clock, "twenty-four/seven"—turning weeks into months and months into "seasons," which make up years. And it was so.

The Almighty made two big lights and they did shine on the earth. The big light, He called the sun and it rested itself over the earth during the day, and the little light, which He called the moon, cruised through the night. The Almighty added little lights called stars and put them in the sky and they did their share of lighting, so that now we have a day and a night for real and the Almighty was feeling mighty fine on the fourth day.

The Almighty then said, "I want the waters to have fish and other kinds of things and I want birds that fill the sky." And He made all them different kinds of living sea things and blessed them. And on the real tip, the Almighty commanded them to "Increase and fill up them waters," and the birds He commanded, "Multiply and fly the earth." And all was done by day five.

Now the Almighty was on the one with his program, replenishing the earth with every kind of animal—cattle and other creeping crawly things, reptiles and so on, and all the beasts like themselves, they were down with the program, too. It just so happened that the Almighty knew His stuff.[2] And He was down with it all, duplicating things and all, and like Hisself He was together with the male; but male and female did He make.

And the Almighty was righteous by them and commanded them to, "Get down with My program and you

---

[2]Genesis, Chapter 1, verses 20 through 26.

will multiply and expand right here on the earth." Each living creature would be on the one with the birds and fish and all the animals. He admonished each of them to be hip to the fact that "These plants will hang tough with fruit for plenty of good eating." He was on the up-and-up with everything He had made and took care of what was His.

And the Almighty looked at the things on His program, liked what He saw and when the nighttime was down again, it was the sixth day.

The Beginning of Man

The Almighty finally finished making the earth and was right on target with all that He had made. So on the big seven, the Almighty said, "Enough!" And the Almighty caused this day to be a special day 'cuz this was the day He'd finished His program.

And this was what went down with the Almighty's program. Now at first things hadn't been too cool, 'cuz plants didn't grow with no H_2O 'round and there was no one hipped to plant raising. But suddenly there was this mist that came from the ground and it watered down the earth, every square inch. And the Almighty created the brother from the dust of the ground and breathed heavily through his nose so that the brother was all the way live; and the brother became a human being.

The Almighty, He made a garden on the east side of Eden and the brother's crib was there and all. And the plants and trees that were good to look at grew. The Tree of Life grew, too, right in the heart of the garden (this was the tree 'tween bad and good). A river from Eden went around watering down the garden and then it divvied up into four parts.[3]

The Almighty made the brother get down with his gig and take care of the garden. And the brother was told he could munch on every tree in the garden, "But be cool 'round the tree of knowledge. Please don't eat from it or you'll die."

And the Almighty felt it wasn't cool for the brother to be by hisself. "I'll make him someone to keep time with," God said. So he started forming every kind of animal out of the ground and brought 'em around to Adam (that was the brother's name) to see what he'd name them. And the brother was down with some great names for the animals, but he was still lonely. So the Almighty put the brother deep in a coma and took out a rib and sealed the place up again. And from the rib He created a sister and brought her down to the brother.

"Right-on," said Adam. "This is my woman 'cuz she's part of me, the man." And that's why she's called woman 'cuz she was made from the rib of man. And this is also why when a brother and sister get together he leaves his mother and father and belongs to her. The brother and sister weren't hipped to the fact that they didn't have no clothes on neither, so this didn't faze them.

---

[3] See Genesis, Chapter 2.

The Sinning Place

Now the serpent was one bad dude, one of the baddest of all the animals the Almighty had made. And the serpent spoke to the sister and asked, "You mean the Almighty told you not to eat of all these trees in the garden?"

And the sister told him, "Yeah, snake, I can eat of these trees, just not the tree of knowledge or the Almighty said I'd be knocked off."

And that bad ol' serpent told the sister, "Nah, sister, he's feeding you a line of bull. You won't die. The Almighty just knows that if you eat from the tree you'll be hipped to what's going down."

So the sister looked back at the tree and saw that things looked righteous and she also wanted to be hipped to what was going down, so she dug in and gave some to her old man to eat.

And quick as a flash they got hipped to the fact that they didn't have on no clothes so they put together some fig leaves for some appropriate threads. Soon they both heard the voice of the Almighty walking 'round in the garden, so they took to hiding from the presence of the Almighty.

The Almighty was cool, though. He walked through the garden knowing what had gone down already. He called out for Adam and the sister. And the brother yelled out that he wasn't dressed, but the truth be told, he was just plain scared.[4]

---

[4]The story of Adam and Eve is found in Genesis, Chapter 3.

And the Almighty asked, "What's up, brother? Who hipped you to the fact you don't have on any clothes? You been eating from the tree I specifically told you not to touch?"

And the brother answered, "Well, yeah, that's true. You see, my ol' lady gave me some and I ate it."

The Almighty then turned to the sister, "Girl, what have you done?"

And the sister said, "The serpent talked me into it and I ate it."

So the Almighty said to the serpent, "Boy, you messed up! I'm gonna curse you worse than all the cattle and every other animal on earth. You'll crawl 'round on your belly for this (at the time the snake stood upright) and eat dust. And the sister won't be able to stand the sight of you, you wretched creature, nor you her and your kids and her kids will feel 'bout the same. The sister'll be scared of you and so will her kids. But you'll be scared of them, too, as will your kids. They'll beat you 'cross the head and you'll try and bite their heels."

Then the Almighty said to the sister, "Your turn. When you have babies, you'll be hurtin' worse than you can imagine, but even so you'll still want to get soul to soul with your ol' man and have other babies. And by the way, your ol' man is your boss."

To Adam He said, "'Cuz you listened to your ol' lady and didn't do what I told you to, you'll have it hard, man. You won't be able to make a decent living on this land. It'll grow stickers and weeds and you'll be eating plenty grass just to keep yourself going. And 'til your dying day, you'll sweat and slave over this land and then when you're gone, you'll go back to the very ground I made you from."

The brother named his ol' lady Eve ('cuz it means the one who gives life) and he said, "The sister shall be the mother of all brotherhood."   The Almighty then gave Adam and his ol' lady some clothes made from animal skins.

And now the Almighty spoke aloud, "Now that Adam is as hipped to good and bad as We are, suppose he gets hipped to the tree of life and lives forever?"   So to remedy that, the Almighty made the brother leave the Garden of Eden forever and a day, and made him farm other ground.   Right then and there Adam and Eve were evicted and the Almighty set angels to guard the east side of Eden with a flaming sword so that they couldn't get in the front door to reach the Tree of Life.

Cain Wastes Abel

Now you gotta understand that Adam and Eve got together so that Eve had a baby boy who she named Cain (meaning "I made him").   Her reason was simple, "With the Almighty's help I've made a boy."   Her next kid was a brother for Cain who she named Abel.

Abel took care of sheep and Cain was a farmer.   When the harvest came, Cain brought the Almighty a gift from what he'd planted.   Abel, on the other hand, brought the choicest cuts from his best lamb and gave them to the Almighty.   And the Almighty felt Abel's gift was right-on, but not Cain's.   Cain got bent out of shape about it, and his nose was wide open with jealousy.

"What's up with you?" asked the Almighty.   "Why the long face?"   And He admonished Cain, "Look, man.

Things could be real cool if you'd straighten up, but if you don't watch it, bad things will happen. You can handle this if you want to."[5]

One day Cain asked his brother to join him in the fields for a walk and as they were walking along the way, Cain hit his brother in the head and wasted him.

Afterwards the Almighty asked Cain, "Where's your brother, man? You know—Abel?"

And Cain snarled, "Look, man. What am I, his keeper or something? You think I keep him in my back pocket?"

But the Almighty already knew the score and He was hip to the fact that Abel was dead. "You've been busted, boy. What have you tried to get away with? Don't you know that Abel's blood is crying to me from the ground." And the Almighty ordered Cain to "Get away from here and don't come back. By the way, there'll be no more crops for you no matter how long or hard you work. And you're a fugitive, man—on the run and an outsider on this earth, just drifting from place to place."

And Cain pleaded with the Almighty, "Hey, man. Don't do this. You know I can't handle that. You've made me into a convict and everybody will be wanting to blow me away."

But the Almighty was ready for that and said, "They ain't gonna do nothing to you, man, 'cuz whatever happens to you will happen to them seven times over." And then the Almighty placed a mark on Cain so folks

---

[5]The Almighty warns Cain in Genesis, Chapter 4.

would know not to blow him away. Cain went away and settled down in a town called Nod, just east of Eden.

Cain and his ol' lady had a baby, naming him Enoch. The place where Cain set up stakes was also named Enoch for his kid. And after that it was on 'cuz Cain's family grew and grew. His sons and their sons had lots of kids, some becoming the first musicians. These folks jammed with the harp and the flute, while another branch of the family made some way-out brass and iron.

Later, Eve had a baby named Seth (meaning "Granted") 'cuz as Eve said, "The Almighty has blessed me with another boy for the one Cain blew away." When Seth became a man, he had a boy and named him Enosh. And it was this point in time that folks started calling themselves "brothers in the Lord."

And the roots of Adam—a brother made by the Almighty at the beginning of His program—were larger than life. The Almighty created the brother and sister and was righteous by them in that the brother was made in the image of the Almighty.

Adam was 130 years old when he sired Seth, his boy, who was the spitting image of hisself. When Seth was born, Adam dealt with life another 800 years and had other sons and daughters. He lived to be 930.

Finally, many years passed and one of Adam's descendants, a brother named Noah, came on the scene to do a job for the Almighty like never before.

Noah Spells Relief

Now it was at this time that people were all over the place filling the earth up and spirits from the spirit world saw all those beautiful sisters and took any they liked as their women. The Almighty Himself said, "The brother has become evil and he can't continue to worry my Spirit. I'll give him just 120 years to straighten up and fly right."

The evil spirits from the spirit world got down with the earth sisters and stories were told then and even now about their children who were called giants. When the Almighty saw just how far the wickedness of the world had gone, doing all sorts of evil and bad things, He was sorry He'd gone that far with His program. It just broke Him up.[6]

And He said, "I'll have to get rid of these creatures I've made. Even the birds and the other animals, too. I'm sorry I even made them."

But one brother, Noah, was a real joy to the Almighty. Here is the story about Noah:

Noah was the only real brother living on the earth at this time. He was a cool brother who lived according to the Almighty's rules and regulations. And he had three sons— Shem, Ham and Japheth.

Meanwhile things were getting out of hand and the Almighty was really upset with all the things going down 'round Him.

---

[6]The story of Noah and the flood can be found in Genesis, Chapters 5 through 8.

So while the Almighty was hipped to what was going down, He told Noah that because of these hard times He was gonna get rid of the world. "I'm fed up, Noah, with what's happenin' 'round here. These folks ain't what's happenin' anymore, so I'm gonna do what I gotta do, and end things once and for all. Man, I'm gonna blow the brothers clear outta the water. Here's what I want you to do: "Get some wood that's thick and seal it with tar. Do as I tell you now; make decks and stalls throughout. I want it 450 feet long, 75 feet wide and 45 feet high with a skylight that'll go 'round the ship, eighteen inches below the roof; then make three decks like I showed you and put a door in the side."

The Almighty wanted Noah to be prepared for what was going down. "I'm gonna cover the earth with tons of water and everything—I mean everything—I've made will die. But if you do like I tell you, everybody in your ship will be saved; your wife and your sons and their wives. Next, I want you to bring some animals, both male and female, into the boat; birds, reptiles, one of each. Then store away all the food you'll need."

And it was a done deal with Noah 'cuz he did what the Almighty had said.

And the Waters Came Coursing Down

So the day came when the Almighty said to Noah, "It's time, Noah. Go into the ship just as I've told you to. And I'm doing this 'cuz you're a right-on-time brother. Bring in the animals, just like I told you, a pair each, except the ones that you'll either be eating or sacrificing. For them I want you to take seven pairs. That way there'll be every kind of life to reproduce when the flood is over." Next the Almighty laid the timetable down for Noah, "One week from now I'll start the rains and it'll rain forty days and nights and everything else I've made will die."

And the brother was truly right-on with the Almighty and did exactly as he was told to do. Noah was 600 when the flood came. Noah, his wife, his sons and their wives, and animals and food were loaded into the ship to get away from the flood. He had all kinds of animals; the ones for eating and sacrifice and those that were not and the birds and reptiles. They came on board, just like the Almighty had said.

So on the 600th year, second month, and seventeenth day of Noah's life, the water came down. But Noah had already gone in the boat with his family like the Almighty had told him to. He and his family went on board with the animals as the Almighty said: two by two, they came, male and female. And the Almighty, His own self, shut the door of that great ship real tight and sealed them in.

For forty days the rains came, continuing 'til they covered the ground and it lifted the boat high above the waters. The waters rose covering mountains and lifting the boat higher and higher. The waters rose more than twenty-two feet above the highest peaks of any mountain. And everything and everybody not on that boat, every living thing, died. For 150 days the water covered the earth.

Rain, Rain Go Away

But the Almighty kept Noah and every other living thing on the boat constant on His mind. He sent winds to blow 'cross the waters and make them disappear after the rains stopped and the gushes of water upon the earth had ceased. And 150 days after the flood started, the boat rested itself on the mountain of Ararat. The waters continued to go down into the ground and three months later other mountain tops could be seen. And still another forty days passed before Noah opened a hole in the ship to let out a raven to fly 'round for dry land. He also sent out a dove, but the dove found not a drop of dry land and came back to Noah. Noah took the dove back in.

Still another seven days passed before Noah sent out the dove again and this time the dove returned with an olive leaf and Noah knew that the water was almost down. And still another week passed before Noah sent out the dove again and this time she didn't come back.

It was twenty-nine days before Noah got up enough nerve to open the door and this time when he looked, the water was gone. It took another eight weeks for the earth to dry, though. Leaving in pairs and groups, everybody on the boat left, 'cuz the Almighty said it was alright.

Noah built an altar and sacrificed some of the animals that the Almighty had told him to bring. The Almighty was happy about the sacrifice and said to Himself, "I'll never lay another hand on the earth with a flood, even though brothers will do wrong." And He looked out on what He had made and said, "As long as the earth stays around, there'll be springtime and summer, winter and fall, day and night—twenty-four/seven, just like it was."

The Rainbow Connection

The Almighty was right by Noah and blessed him and his family, imploring them to "Go out and multiply." The Almighty explained to Noah that the animals would be afraid of them 'cuz He had given Noah and his family power over them to be used for food. "I've also given you grain and vegetables." But the Almighty warned them not to eat any animals unless the blood that flows through them has been drained off. And his rules were simple. "Knocking folks off would be a crime and would not be tolerated. Any man-killing animal should be wasted. Any brother who kills another brother who has been made in my image shall also die. But I do want you to get on with the program now, and replenish the earth."

Then the Almighty made His promise to Noah and his family: "I promise with My heart that I will never again destroy your earth with water. And with this promise comes a sign: In the clouds will be a rainbow at the end of the rains that touch the earth. From the clouds to the earth's surface, a rainbow will be the sign and remind Me never to lay a finger on this earth again with floods. I'll see that rainbow and remember My promise to you forever and a day."

Noah had three boys named Shem, Ham and Japheth.[7] The nations of the earth came from Noah's three boys.

Noah became a farmer and planted a vineyard and made wine. One day he drank too much and lay 'round his tent without a stitch on. Ham the father of Canaan, saw

---

[7]Ham is the ancestor of the Canaanites

his father without any clothes on and went and told his other brothers. Now Shem and Japheth got a robe and walked backwards into the tent so that they wouldn't see their daddy naked and covered him up. Noah was really mad after he sobered up and found out what had happened, so he laid a heavy trip on Ham and cursed his future generation. "I swear," said Noah, "that the future generations of Ham shall be slaves and lowest of slaves, at that." And to the future generation of Shem and Japheth he said, "May the Almighty bless both Shem and Japheth and be righteous by them. And may Ham's kids be Shem's slaves and let Japheth share in his riches."

And Noah was 950 years old when he died, living 350 years after the great flood.

A Tower of an Idea

After the flood people talked one kind of talk. That is to say, everybody who was anybody understood exactly what was going down. Soon folks were spread for miles around, mostly eastward 'til they covered all of Babylon.

Now Babylon was kinda bare, so that these folks got a wonderful idea—or so they thought. Everybody started talking about building the baddest building 'round; "one that would reach all the way to heaven," they agreed. It would be a monument to the bad boys who built it.

"If we build it for the homeboys," they said, "we won't be so eager to stray away from the homebase." So they got lots of bricks and tar and started building this great tower.

But the Almighty came down sort of unexpected and looked 'round and saw what was coming down. He said,

"Look! If the brothers are able to pull this off and they're just starting out, just think what else they might try and do. Let's give a group of them a different kind of talk. It'll confuse these brother who wanna be so bad."

And that's exactly what went down. The folks that thought they would be party to building the baddest tower ever went every which way 'cuz they was confused from the different kinds of talk goin' on. They eventually left and went to other parts of the earth.

And all this happened a little bit after the big waters had blown brothers away. In fact, things started over again with Noah's three boys who created this large family. And it was Noah's boy, Shem. who went on to have a laid out relationship with the Almighty.[8]

Abram Leaves Home

One of Shem's descendants was a brother named Terah. Now when Terah died, the Almighty told his boy, Abram, to leave the little town of Haran where he grew up. "I'll show you the way, son, 'cuz there are great plans in store for you. You will be the father of a nation and have many children and blessings. Those that are righteous by you, I'll sho 'nuff be righteous by them. By the same token, if someone decides to curse you, well I'll deal with that too."[9]

---

[8]The descendents of Shem, Noah's son, can be found in Genesis, Chapter 11.

[9]See Genesis, Chapters 12 through 18 for the story of Abraham and the Almighty's promise to him.

So at seventy-five, Abram did what the Almighty said. Lot went with him. He took his wife, Sarai, and all their riches to go from Haran like the Almighty had said.

They went through Canaan and on to a place called Shechem where they set up camp beside an oak tree at Moreh (there were other Canaanites there, too). Then the Almighty appeared before Abram and said, "This land will belong to your family." And Abram built an altar there 'cuz the Almighty had visited that place. Abram continued southward to the hill country between west Bethel and east Ai. He made an altar here too and talked with the Almighty again. He then continued southward to the Negeb, where he laid back for a while.

Abram went further down and ended up in Egypt to live. As he got close to Egypt he laid a heavy trip on his wife, Sarai. "Look, woman. You're a fine looking chick, so I want to let everyone think that you are my sister. Dig?" Sarai nodded. "They might try to kill me if they think I'm your old man to get me out of the way. But if they think you're my sister, well, they'll roll out the carpet for the both of us."

Well, sure enough, all the brothers thought Sarai was really fine. Everywhere she went someone was talking about how fine she was. They told Pharaoh about her. Pharaoh loaded down many gifts to Abram—sheep, oxen, donkeys, men and women slaves, and camels. But the Almighty wasn't pleased with what was happenin' at all. He sent a terrible plague on Pharaoh's home.

Pharaoh called in Abram. "Hey, man. What's up with this? Whatcha tryin' to pull, bringing in your woman and letting folks think she was your sister? What did you expect with her so fine? Look, man. Take your woman and go!" he roared.

So Pharaoh sent Abram and his woman out of his country. And he let him keep everything he'd given him, too.

Abram's New Crib

Abram and his ol' lady left Egypt and headed north to Negeb. He had with him his nephew, Lot, and all his goods. But the new place was not big enough for Abram and his crew. Plenty of fights broke out between herdsmen and Abram's group. You see, the Canaanite brothers and their neighbors, the Perizzite brothers, were all dangerous people. So Abram said to Lot, "Man, we got to figure out a way to stop this fighting 'cuz we just can't afford it. These are our brothers too and we've got to keep unity." So Abram came up with a dynamite plan to stop the fighting. "First, Lot, I want you to figure out which section of the city you want to run. If you take the west, I'll take the east, but if you decide you want the east, well the west is alright by me."

Lot stuck immediately to the idea and decided that the Jordan River area was just right for him. It was like the Garden of Eden, almost, but more like the area around Zoar, near Egypt. So that's the area he chose. He took up his group and took over the place there. And Abram stayed in the land of Canaan, while Lot lived in his Eden-like area near the city of Sodom. The brothers in Sodom were pretty tough, though, and weren't to be messed with. They were so mean that the Almighty called them wicked.

The Almighty came down to have a talk with Abram. "Look around you, man. For as far as your eye can see, that's yours and your kids'. I'm gonna give you so many you won't be able to count 'em. Go 'round and try things out and see just what I'm laying on you." With that said, Abram then moved his household to the oaks of Mamre, near Hebron and built an altar to the Almighty there.

Abram Kicks Some Butt

Now Amraphel was king of Shinar, while Abram was putting up stakes. This place was 'round about Babylon. Anyway, King Amraphel got together with some other kings, including King Chedorlaomer, and went to battle mostly 'cuz he was sick of working and bowing down to King Chedorlaomer for more than thirteen years. (These guys thought things would be different with Chedorlaomer, but it wasn't happenin'.) So these guys took over the Siddim Valley (near the Salt Sea) with their bad armies.

Chedorlaomer and his friends, though, had different ideas. They were gonna show these brothers just who was really king.[10] And they did just that, kicking butt and taking names. However, they made the mistake of taking Abram's nephew, Lot, as well. Bad mistake!

During the battle, one brother managed to escape and tell Abram what had gone down. Abram, you remember,

---

[10]To know more of the history of the kings of Babylon, read Genesis, Chapter 14.

was camped near the oak of Mamre the Amorite (brother of Eshcol and Aner, Abram's friends).

Abram got plenty hot when he learned about his nephew Lot being captured by Chedorlaomer. He got together 318 of his men and ran after the brothers all the way to Dan. During the night he ran right over the tired brothers of Chedorlaomer and got back everything—all Lot's stuff, his women and friends, with Lot leading the pack.

Abram returned victorious after going up against the king of all these uppity valleys, Chedorlaomer and the rest. The King of Sodom was impressed by what Abram had done and Melchizedek, the king of Salem (Jerusalem) brought him wine and bread and blessed him with this blessing:

"May the blessings of the Almighty, Creator of Heaven and Earth, come upon you, man. And a special blessing to Him 'cuz He's the one who delivered you from those crazy hotheads in the Valley."

Then Abram blessed Melchizedek with a tenth of what he had handled.

The King of Sodom just wanted his people back. "Man, just hand over my brothers and you can keep the loot."

But Abram told him, "Listen, man. I've already promised the Almighty I wouldn't take nothing from you 'cuz you might be tempted to say I got rich off you. All I want, man, is the food we've already eaten. But you can divvy up some of this stuff 'tween my friends, Aner, Eshcol and Mamre."

Abram's Pact with the Almighty

Later, when Abram was having his regular talk with the Almighty, he was again blessed. "Don't be scared, Abram, my man. You did right by those folks and I will always defend you. You'll be blessed plenty because of what you did."

But Abram was slightly miffed. "O Lord Almighty, what good is it to be rich and still not have any kids? I have no son, no heir, no one to take my place or take over my riches." He was scared that someone other than his flesh and blood would take over.

The Almighty soothed his fears. "No one's gonna take over what's yours, man. You'll have a son to take over everything. Don't worry."

Then the Almighty brought Abram outside 'neath the stars to look up into the nighttime skies. "Look up, man. See the stars. Boy, you'll have so many generations of people you won't be able to count 'em!" So Abram believed the Almighty's words and the Almighty was happy 'cuz Abram had faith in Him.

And He said, "I am the Almighty, man. I'm the one who brought you out of the city of Ur where the Chaldean brothers ruled and gave you this land forever."

But Abram wondered, "How, God, can I be sure that they'll give it up?" So the Almighty told him to take a three-year-old heifer, a three-year-old female goat, a three-year-old ram, a turtledove and a young pigeon. "Divvy 'em up into halves except the birds." Later, though, when the vultures came down on the carcasses, Abram shooed them away.

That evening Abram had a nightmare, dreaming that something terrible was gonna come down.

The Almighty told him, "Yeah, well something bad will happen. Your descendants will be made into slaves for 'bout 400 years. But don't worry, man, 'cuz I'm gonna come down real hard on the ones that do this to them. In the end, your people will have it all." But the Almighty went on to explain, "You, however, will live to be an old man. Don't you worry 'bout nothing. After 400 years they'll come back to this land 'cuz these bad brothers here won't be ready to go down until then."

And as the sun went down and it turned dark, Abram saw a smoking fire-pot and a flaming torch that passed between the divvied up carcasses and on that day he and the Almighty made their pact. The Almighty then told Abram that he was gonna make a deal with him and give him and all his descendants a lotta land, from the Wadi-el-Arish to the Euphrates River.[11]

The Story of Hagar

Sarai and Abram still didn't have any children, so Sarai gave Abram her maid, an Egyptian sister named Hagar, to be his second wife.

"Since the Almighty hasn't given me a child for you, you can get down with my Egyptian slave and maybe she can give you a baby."

---

[11]Read Genesis, Chapter 15, verse 18 through 21.

And Abram said, "Okay." It had been ten years and he and Sarai hadn't been lucky, so he slept with Hagar and she conceived. When Hagar realized she was pregnant, she held it over her mistress all the time.

Then Sarai said to Abram, "It's all your fault. Now that you got that girl pregnant, she treats me like dirt; like she's got some kind of hold over you. I hope the Almighty gets you for this."

"Look, woman," Abram said. "You can do what you want to that girl. I don't care." So Sarai beat up on Hagar and she ran away. The Almighty's angel ran up on Hagar near a desert spring by the road to Shur and said: "Hagar, Sarai's maid. What's up, girl? Where you headed?"

"I'm getting away from my mistress," replied Hagar.

The angel then said, "Look, go back to your mistress, Hagar, and act the way you're supposed to. You're pregnant and gonna have a son. You should name him Ishmael (meaning "God hears"), because the Almighty has heard your cries. Ishmael will be a wild brother, free and untamed. He will be down on everyone and they'll probably feel likewise towards him, but don't sweat it, 'cuz he'll live among his own brothers."

Later Hagar talked about the Almighty as one who looked after her. "I saw the Almighty," she said, "and lived to tell about it." The well where she saw Him was named "The Well of the Living One Who Sees Me."

So Hagar had a boy for Abram and named him Ishmael. Abram was 86.

Abraham—The Father of Nations

Abram had just turned 99 when the Almighty came to him and said, "I am the Almighty One; do what I say and live as you should. I've made a deal that will give you a mighty nation. You shall have many nations to your name." Abram hit the ground in gratitude for all the Almighty had talked about.

"What's more," the Almighty said, "I'm giving you a new name. It will no longer be Abram, 'Exalted Father,' but Abraham, 'Father of Nations'—'cuz that's what you'll be. I have said it. I will give you millions of children, grandchildren and great-grandchildren and I make this deal forever. I shall be your man and the Almighty of all that is yours. And I will give you all this land of Canaan forever. I will be your God.

"Your part of the deal," the Almighty continued, "is to abide by my rules. You and all yours shall live by this deal we've made: Every brother shall be circumcised (the foreskin of the penis shall be cut off). This will be proof that you accept the deal we've made. After a man child has reached the eighth day of life he shall be circumcised. Every male, including slaves and anyone born in your hometown. This is a real deal, permanent and sealed. All must be circumcised marking this deal closed. Anyone who doesn't deal with what I've laid down shall be cut off from his brothers."

Then the Almighty went on to say, "Sarai shall have a baby for you and her new name will be Sarah, 'Princess,' and she will have riches and many children. Many kings will be part of this brotherhood."

So Abraham threw himself down to worship the Almighty but inside he thought it a joke. "Me, a daddy?" he said in amusement. "Me—100 years old? And my ol' lady, Sarah, at 90? No way!"

So Abraham said to the Almighty, "Yeah, sure Man. Come on and bless Ishmael!"

But the Man would not be laughed at, "You don't understand, man. I said Sarah would give you a son and his name will be Isaac, 'Laughter,' and I'll seal the deal with him, not Ishmael 'cuz he'll receive what's due him, too. In fact twelve princes will make up his tribe. But the deal I'm making is with Isaac, who'll be around here about this time next year."

That ended the talk between Abraham and the Almighty 'cuz that was all He had to say. And on that day Abraham did what the Almighty had said and circumcised all the males of his household. Abraham was 99 and Ishmael was 13 and both of them were circumcised along with the brothers of the household whether born there or bought as slaves.

Abraham's Visitors from Heaven

One laid-back summer afternoon, near the oak grove at Mamre, the Almighty came to Abraham in the form of one of three brothers. Abraham noticed them when he was sitting outside his tent cooling down. He sprang up to meet them and welcome them in.

"Brothers," he said, "please don't go any further. Stop and rest your bones while I get some water to cool your feet down. Stay awhile and rest before you get on with your travels."

"Okay, brother," they answered. "We'll do as you say."

Then Abraham ran over to his woman imploring, "Sarah, fix up some pancakes and use your best stuff. Make it enough for three hungry brothers." Then he ran down to the herd and selected a fat calf and told a servant to hurry and butcher it. Soon he had a feast fit for a king and set it before the three brothers beneath the trees and they ate.

"Where is Sarah, your lady?" they asked.

"In the tent," said Abraham.

Then one of the brothers (who was really the Almighty) said, "Next year you and Sarah will have a son." Sarah was listening in from inside. She and Abraham were both old folks and she was past the prime for having a baby.

So she laughed to herself, "A woman my age having a baby? And with my man so old himself."

Then the Almighty said to Abraham, "Why is Sarah laughing? Why did she say 'A woman my age having a baby?' Is there anything I can't do? Just wait and see, brother, 'cuz Sarah will have a son for you."

But Sarah said, "I wasn't laughing," 'cuz she was scared.

The men ate their meal and then started towards Sodom; Abraham went part way with them.

"Should we let Abraham know what's goin down?" the Almighty asked. "'Cuz Abraham will be the source of all future brotherhood. I have singled him out to have a good and righteous household—brothers just and good—so that I do what I said I would."

So the Almighty said to Abraham, "I have heard that the people of Sodom and Gomorrah are some real mean dudes and that everything they do goes down wrong. I'm going down there to see whether these reports are on time. Then I will know what to bring on them." While the other two brothers went on towards the city, the Almighty stayed around Abraham for a spell. And Abraham asked him, "Will you do away with the good and bad brothers there? Suppose you find fifty good brothers—will you be down with them all? That couldn't be right, man. Why should the good and bad go down together?"

And the Almighty replied, "If I find fifty good brothers there I will spare the whole city."

And Abraham said, "Look, man, I know I'm only dust and ashes but just take for instance, you find only forty-five. Will you destroy the city for lack of just five brothers?"

And the Almighty said, "Okay, brother. If I find forty-five I won't destroy the city."

And Abraham said, "But suppose there's only forty?"

And the Almighty said, "Okay, man. Forty!"

Abraham approached the Almighty again. "Don't be angry with me, man. But suppose you find only thirty?"

"Okay, thirty," the Almighty agreed.

But Abraham grew frantic. "Suppose you find only twenty."

"Then twenty," the Almighty said patiently.

Finally Abraham implored Him, "How about ten?"

And the Almighty said, "Okay, Abraham, ten." And the Almighty then went down to Sodom and Gomorrah and Abraham went to his tent.

Seeing Is Believing

Evening time brought the two angels to the city's entrance and Lot was sitting there when they came. When he saw them he stood up to meet and welcome them.[12]

"Brothers," he said, "come to my house as my guests for tonight. You can sleep as long as you like and be on your way tomorrow."

"No thanks, brother," they said. "We'll just stretch out here on the streets."

But Lot would have it his way and insisted that the brothers come home with him and he fed them and when they were about down for the night some punks from the streets yelled from outside to Lot, "Hey, man, bring those guys out. We want to party with them and get down."

Lot tried to talk with them. "Look, brothers, I can't let you do that. Listen, I have two virgin daughters and I'll surrender them to you but leave these brothers alone, okay?"

So one punk yelled to the others, "Who does he think he is; trying to tell us what to do. Keep this up, man, and we'll do to you what we've planned for them." And then they pushed Lot out of the way and broke down the door.

But the two brothers inside heard the commotion and pulled Lot in and shut the door tight. They then blinded the brothers outside so they couldn't find the door.

"What relatives you got inside the city?" the men asked. "Get them out of this place—you and your sons, daughters, family, all of them for we intend to destroy this place. The

---

[12]Sodom and Gomorrah destroyed. Genesis, Chapter 19.

smell of this dog haven has reached heaven and the Almighty is plenty mad about what's been going down."

So Lot ran out and told his daughters and their husbands to get out of town, fast, 'cuz the Almighty was coming down with something fierce. But they were fools and didn't listen.

At dawn the angels got antsy. "Look, man. You gotta hurry. Take your wife and two daughters who are here and get out of town while you can or you'll fry, too. You don't want no part of this."

When Lot didn't move fast enough, the angels seized his hand and the hands of his woman and two daughters and headed them to safety, for the Almighty was on their side.

"Run for your lives, man," the angels said. "And don't look back. Run to the mountains for if you stay down here you'll be wiped out."

"Please, mister. Don't make me go up in the mountains. See that little city over there. It's close," Lot implored. "I'll be safe there, man. Please!"

"Okay, man," the angel said. "I can deal with that, but hurry up. I can't do nothing until you move, man. So move!" The little city was later named Zoar, which literally means "little city."

It was just past dawn when Lot reached the village and as he got there the Almighty's hand was heavy with fire and flaming tar from heaven on the cities of Sodom and Gomorrah, destroying everything in the way. And Lot's ol' lady looked back on what was going down and she was turned into salt.

Abraham himself heard all that was going down and when he looked out across the plains all he saw was smoldering flames and rubble. But the Almighty had listened to Abraham's plea and saved Lot and his family from the destruction in Sodom and Gomorrah.

Later, Lot left Zoar 'cuz he was scared of the people 'round there and went and lived in a cave in the mountains with his two daughters. One day the older sister said to the younger, "There are no brothers here and no one Dad would let us marry anyway. Soon he'll be too old to have kids, so let's sleep with our ol' man so that we won't be wiped out as a clan." And that night they got him drunk and the older sister went and got busy with her dad, but he didn't know it.

The next morning the older sister said, "Look, girlfriend, I slept with dad and tonight we'll get him drunk again and you get down with him." So they got him drunk again and the younger sister lay with him. He didn't raise an eyebrow and they both got pregnant for their father and the older sister's baby was named Moab and he became the father of the Moabites. The name of the younger sister's baby was Ben Ammi and he became the father of the nation of Ammonites.

Abraham Up Against a Wall

Abraham continued south to Negeb and settled between Kadesh and Shur. One day when he visited the city of Gerar he told everyone that Sarah was his sister. So King Abimelech sent for her and brought her to his house.

But the Almighty came to him in a dream and said, "You're a dead man, son. That woman you took is married."

King Abimelech had not gotten down with her yet, so he begged the Almighty, "Look, man. I ain't slept with the lady yet. Abraham told me she was his sister. How was I to know? I didn't want to do anything wrong."

"Yes, I know, man," said the Almighty. "That's why I didn't let you do nothing wrong. Now take her back to her ol' man and I will pray for you and you'll live. But if you don't do this, you will be wiped out permanently."

The king got busy and called his household together and told 'em what had gone down and they got scared.

Next the king called in Abraham. "What's up with this, man? What did I ever do to you? Just who do you think you are?"

"Sorry, man," said Abraham. "Listen, we got here and I got a little scared, you know. I thought, 'This is a godless place and if they think she's my ol' lady, they'll kill me.' And anyway she is my half sister so I said to her, 'Listen, woman, tell the folks that you are my sister,' and she did."

So King Abimelech took sheep and oxen and servants and gave them to Abraham along with his ol' lady. And he said to Abraham, "You decide any place in my kingdom you want to live and it's yours, okay?" And to Sarah he said, "I'm gonna lay a thousand silver pieces on you for any embarrassment you might have. Now I've set things right."

And Abraham prayed to the Almighty and asked him to cure the king and his women 'cuz the Almighty had laid barrenness on the women to deal with them for taking Abraham's ol' lady.

The Birth of Isaac

The Almighty kept his word and Sarah got pregnant. She gave birth to a baby boy in Abraham's old age, when the Almighty said; and Abraham named him Isaac ('cuz that means "laughter"). Eight days later Abraham circumcised him just like the Almighty had told him to. Abraham was 100 years old.

And Sarah said, "God has brought me laughter. All who hear me will be happy with me. Who would've thought I could have a baby for my ol' man? I gave my man a child when he was 100 years old."

After a spell the child grew and no longer nursed at his momma's breast, so Abraham gave a party. But Sarah noticed Ishmael (the boy of Abraham and the Egyptian sister, Hagar) teasing Isaac and she got bent out of shape tellin' her ol' man, "Get rid of that slave girl and her boy. I don't want him sharing anything with my boy. I won't deal with it."

But the Almighty told Abraham not to worry about his slave wife and her boy. "Go ahead, Abraham, do what your wife wants 'cuz Isaac is the one that I made my promise. Don't worry about anything 'cuz they'll have what's theirs and it's really not your business anymore."

So Abraham gets up early the next morning and sends Hagar and Ishmael away after he put together food and water for them. Hagar went out to Beersheba, not knowing where she was going, just walking around. When the water was gone, she put the kid down and walks away saying, "I don't want to watch him die." Then she lay in the dirt crying.

But the Almighty was watching everything as it went down and sent an angel to Hagar. "Hagar, what's the matter with you? Look, the Almighty is watching out for you. Go on to your boy and put your arms 'round him. The Almighty will make a nation from his blood."

So Hagar went to her boy and before her very eyes she saw a well and filled her water jug. And the Almighty was right by Ishmael. He grew up in the country and became a dynamite teacher. And later when he was a grown man, his mother put together a marriage for him with an Egyptian sister.

Around this time King Abimelech and Phicol, who commanded the king's troops, went over to Abraham and said to him, "Look, I can see where the Almighty deals straight up with you. He helps you in every way. Swear to me, Abraham, that you won't try and get over on me or my son or grandson, but that you'll deal straight with me like I've done with you."

Abraham agreed, saying, "Alright, I swear." Then he told the king about a well that the king's people had taken from them with force.

"Hey, man. It's the first I've heard of it," said the king. "I don't know who would do this. Why didn't you lay this on me before, man?"

Abraham shrugged it off by bringing sheep and oxen to the king to show that the deal had been made. He then took seven ewe lambs and set them off to the side. "What's up, man?" the king wanted to know.

"These are my personal gifts to you to square things 'tween us," Abraham told him. "And to point out that this well is mine."

So from that time the well was called Beersheba (it means "Well of the Oath") because this was the place where the king and Abraham squared things. So King Abimelech and his man, Phicol, head of the army, left. And Abraham planted a tamarisk tree beside the well and there he bowed to the Almighty who not only blessed the deal that was made, but witnessed everything that went down. Abraham lived in the Philistine country for a long time.

A Test of Faith

The Almighty tested Abraham's faith and obedience.

"Abraham," called the Almighty.

"What's happenin', Lord," replied Abraham.

"I want you to take Isaac, your beloved son, and go to the land of Moriah and sacrifice him as a burnt offering on one of the mountains which I'll show you."

The next morning Abraham got up, chopped wood for a fire, put a saddle on his donkey and took Isaac and two young brothers up to the place where the Almighty directed. On the third day, Abraham saw the place far away.

"Stay here with the mule," Abraham told the brothers. "Isaac and I will travel over there and then come back."

Abraham made Isaac carry the wood on his shoulders and he carried the knife and flint for making the fire. And the two of them went up together.

"Father," Isaac asked, "we have everything to make the fire, but nothing to sacrifice. Where is the lamb?"

"The Almighty will make things right, son," said Abraham. And up they went.

When they got to the place above where the Almighty told them to go, Abraham built an altar, put the wood down, made the fire, and then tied up his son Isaac, and laid him on the altar. And just when Abraham was going to put the knife in his son's chest and kill him, the Angel of the Almighty shouted down to him. "Abraham! Abraham!"

"Yes, Lord," he answered.

"Put down your knife, man. It's okay. Now I know how much you care for the Almighty. For you would not even hold back someone you love from Him."

Abraham noticed a ram caught by the horns in a bush. He took the ram and sacrificed it instead of his boy. He named the place, "God provides"—and it is called that to this day.

Then the Angel of the Almighty called down to Abraham again. "Because you didn't hold nothing back from Him, not even your son, the Almighty promises to give you big things." And the Almighty said, "I will bless you many times over and your blood shall survive through the ages. These brothers will be so bad that they'll handle their enemies with ease—all because you obeyed me."

So Abraham and Isaac returned to the brothers down below and went back to Beersheba.

Later a message came from his hometown that one of Abraham's brothers, Nahor, now had eight sons.[13]

The Death of Sarah

Sarah was 127 when she died in Hebron in the land of Canaan. Abraham was so heartbroken over her death that he cried. Standing by her body, he said to the brothers of Heth: "Here I am, a visitor in a strange land, with no place to bury my wife. Please sell me a piece of land to bury her."

"Sure," the brothers replied. "Look, Abraham. You're an okay brother with the Almighty and it'll be an honor to have you choose the finest burial ground we have so you can bury her."

Abraham bowed low before them and said, "Since this is how you feel, please ask Ephron, Zohar's son, to sell me the cave of Machpelah, down there at the end of this field. I'll lay out the full price, whatever is agreed on, and it will become a permanent cemetery for my family."

But Ephron wouldn't hear of Abraham buying anything. "No, man, listen. I give you the field and the cave. In front of everybody, I give it to you. Bury your dead!"

"If you will give it," said Abraham, "let me pay you. Then I will bury my dead."

---

[13]From these boys descended the sister who would grow up to marry Abraham's son, Isaac. See Genesis, Chapter 22, verses 20 through 24.

So Ephron told him that the land was worth four hundred shekels of silver.[14] "But what is money between us?" said Ephron. "Whatever. Just bury your dead."

And Abraham gave the shekels of silver to Ephron for the land which was in Machpelah, which was before Mamre; the field and the cave and all the trees that were in the field. Ephron deeded the land to Abraham and Abraham buried Sarah his wife there in the field and the cave which were deeded to Abraham for a burial place.

Isaac Gets a Wife

Now Abraham was old and up in age; and the Lord had blessed Abraham in many ways. And Abraham spoke to the oldest servant who served and ran his house, "Place your hand under my thigh." And then Abraham made him swear that he would not look for a wife for his son from among the Canaanites where they lived, but would instead get a homegirl for his son, Isaac, who was of his kind. But his servant wished to know what would happen should this homegirl not want to travel from her home town to where they now lived, and Abraham said if no homegirl wanted to come, he would release the servant from his vow, but made him promise not to take his son there. "It was the Almighty, maker of the heavens, who swore to me that he would give this land to my kin from generation to generation. The Lord's angel will guide you to my home town to find a wife for my son."

---

[14]Shekels were the currency for these times.

"And if the woman doesn't want to hang out here, you're released from your oath." The servant put his hand under his master's thigh and swore.

The servant took ten of his master's camels and left. He went to Mesopotamia, to the city of Nahor. There he made the camels kneel down outside the city by a well of water around the time that the women went to get water. And he prayed, "O Lord God of my master Abraham, help me do this. Make it alright."

" 'Cuz I'm standing here by the well of waters and many fine sisters of the men of this city will come to get water. Now let one of the sisters who I'll say, 'Please put your pitcher in so that I can have some water,' tell me to 'drink.' But let her add that she'll also give my camels some water, too. Let her be the one."

And before he'd even finished talking, Rebekah, who was the daughter of Bethuel, making her Abraham's niece, came outside with a pitcher on her shoulder. Now Rebekah was one fine sister, really beautiful, and a virgin since no man had been down with her. Rebekah came to the well to fill up her pitcher.

Abraham's servant met her there. "Please, let me have some water from your pitcher."

She replied, "Drink, my lord." And she placed her pitcher down and gave him some water. And when the servant had quenched his thirst, Rebekah asked if she could give some water to his camels as well.

Rebekah furnished water for the camels and the servant was wondering if the sister was indeed the one. When the camels had finished, the servant took a golden nose ring worth half a shekel, and two bracelets for her wrists worth ten shekels of gold and asked, "Whose daughter are you? Do you think there's room there at your father's house?"

She told him, "I am the daughter of Bethuel, Milcah's son, who she had for Nahor. Sure, we've plenty of room for you to stay." And the servant was down with some real worshipping to the Almighty saying, "Blessed be the Lord, God of my master Abraham, who has not forgotten my master. And Lord, thanks, 'cuz you've led me to the house of my master's brothers."

And Rebekah ran and told her kinfolks of the man, and Rebekah's brother, whose name was Laban, ran back to the man at the well. Hearing what his sister said, and seeing the nose ring and bracelets on his sister's arm, Laban went to check the servant out. And he said, "Come on in! Bless the Lord, man. Don't just stand there, there's plenty room for you and your camels."

Abraham's servant came to the crib of Laban where he unloaded the camels and the camels were fed and taken care of. And then food was set before the servant, but he would not eat until he had told everyone why he was there.

"I'm Abraham's servant and my master is loaded. God has really blessed him and he has become great. There are flocks and herds, silver and gold, male and female servants, and camels and donkeys. And Sarah, who was my master's wife, had a baby for him when she was old and he was already very rich. Now my master says, 'I don't want my son marrying any of these sisters from the Canaanites, where I live.' He wanted me to come to his father's hometown and find a wife for his son.

"I told him that maybe a sister from his home town would not follow me, but he said that the Lord would provide. He wanted a sister from his home town for his son and that's why I'm here.

"If I can't fulfill this promise to my master, I'm released from my promise to find Isaac a wife from here. So, when I came into town, I asked the Almighty to show me a sign and help me keep my promise to my master." And he recalled to them the story of how if a woman gave him something to drink and then asked to give his camels something to drink, that she would be the one. "And when I asked who she was, she told me that she was the daughter of Bethuel, Nahor's son, who was born to Milcah and I put the nose ring on her nose and the bracelets on her wrists. And I thanked the Lord of my master, Abraham, who led me here.

"Now if you will deal straight with me, and on the up and up with my master, let me know how things are."

Then Laban and Bethuel said, "This is truly a miracle of God. We can't tell you how things are, only God can. Look, here's our sister Rebekah. Take her and go so that she can be your master's son's wife. I think the Almighty has made it pretty clear."

So the servant took Rebekah, but not before laying some gold and silver on Rebekah, along with a new set of threads. He also gave precious things to Rebekah's brother and mother. And later the men and women ate and drank and stayed up all night. In the morning, they got up and asked to be on their way to Abraham. But Rebekah's mother and brother wanted to spend a little time with their sister, at least ten days.

But the servant didn't want to waste any time, so they all decided to let Rebekah decide.

"You want to go with him, now?" they asked. And she said, "I will go."

So Rebekah started on her way to become Isaac's wife. She took with her a nurse to ride with Abraham's servant and his men. And they said to their sister:

"Sister girl, may you become the mother of thousands. And may all of your children possess the gates of those who hate them."

Then Rebekah and her maids went with them and they left. Isaac was living in the south and came by way of Beer Lahai Roi, and went out to meditate in the field that evening. And he looked up and saw the servant coming with Rebekah. Rebekah saw Isaac as well and asked who he was. "It is my master," said the servant and so she took a veil and covered herself. And the servant told Isaac all the things that he had done and Isaac brought her into his mother's tent and got busy, so that she became his wife. And he loved her so that it comforted him after his mother had died.

The Death of Abraham

After Sarah's death, Abraham took another wife named Keturah. And she had children for Abraham as well, but Abraham gave almost everything he owned to Isaac. He also gave gifts to the sons of his concubines and while he was alive, he sent them to the eastern countries, away from his son, Isaac. And his son Ishmael, whose mother was Hagar, the Egyptian, had many descendants to carry on his family name.

Here is the total of Abraham's life 'cuz he lived to be one hundred and seventy-five years. Then Abraham died. He was an old man and full of years and was mourned by his brothers.

And brothers Isaac and Ishmael buried Abraham in the cave of Machpelah, where they had also buried their mother, Sarah, who was Abraham's wife.

After Abraham's death, Isaac was blessed by the Almighty and lived at Beer Lahai Roi. Ishmael lived to be one hundred and thirty-seven years and died. He lived in Havilah as far as Shur (east of Egypt just before you get to Assyria). He died among his brothers.

And Isaac's family tree was such: Isaac was forty years old when he took Rebekah as his wife who was his father's niece, daughter of Bethuel. Now Rebekah hadn't given Isaac any children and Isaac pleaded with the Almighty so that Rebekah could conceive and she did, but she was having a hard time. "What's happenin' with me," she implored of God. And the Almighty said to her:

"Two nations are inside of you. Two homeboys shall be separated from your body; and one homeboy shall be stronger than the other and the older shall serve the younger."

So Rebekah had twins and the first was born red all over. He was like a hairy garment, and they called him Esau. And as Esau was born, his brother took hold of the bottom of Esau's foot, so that his name was called Jacob. And Isaac was sixty years old when Rebekah had the babies.

As the brothers grew, Esau was a really tough hunter, a man of the field, but Jacob was kinda nerdy, living in tents. And Isaac loved Esau because he ate the meat Esau killed, but Rebekah loved Jacob.

Now Jacob cooked a stew and Esau, who had been out in the field, came in real tired. And Esau said to Jacob, "Please give me something to eat, 'cuz I'm so tired."

But Jacob cut a deal. "Look, man. If you're so hungry, sell me your heritage." And Esau who was so hungry he thought he'd die, said, "What good is a heritage if I'm dead, so no problem." Then Jacob asked him to "Swear it, man," and Esau sold his birthright to Jacob. Jacob fed his brother stew, bread, and lentils and Esau did eat. That's how Esau gave away his heritage.

Checking It Out in Gerar

There was famine everywhere, so Isaac went to King Abimelech of the Philistines in Gerar. And the Almighty appeared to Isaac and admonished him not to go into Egypt. He asked him to stay in this land for a while and "I will bless you and your heirs as I promised your ol' man, Abraham.

"There will be plenty of children in your future, and I will give you and your heirs the deal of deals. You see Abraham was cool and straight with me. He kept my orders, my commands, my statutes, and my laws."

So Isaac stayed in the city of Gerar.

The brothers in Gerar kept checking out Isaac's ol' lady, so Isaac told 'em Rebekah was his sister since he thought they might be jealous and kill him if she were his ol' lady. But as King Abimelech was scoping out the situation, he saw Isaac grooving with Rebekah and told him, "Hey, man. She is obviously your ol' lady. How could you jock us and tell us she was your sister?"

So Isaac said, "I was scared, man. I thought someone might knife me if they thought she was my ol' lady."

"Man, what's up with that? You coulda got someone in trouble. Suppose somebody had knocked boots with your wife. How would you have felt? Look, I'll handle this." And with this King Abimelech told his homeboys not to touch the woman as she was really Isaac's ol' lady and anybody jocking 'em would die.

Isaac set up shop in the city of Gerar and made money a hundred times over. The Almighty blessed him. Isaac continued earning money and earned so much money that he had cattle and servants. But the Philistines were jealous.

Now the Philistines had stopped up the wells on Isaac's father's servant's place which were dug in the time of Abraham. The Philistines loaded the wells with dirt.

King Abimelech asked Isaac to leave, "Please, man." He thought that Isaac was much stronger than he was, so Isaac left and stayed 'round the Valley of Gerar where he dug wells like his father had done. And Isaac's servants dug in the valley and found running water. But the herdsmen of Gerar said that the water was theirs and they were ready to throw down for it. So Isaac called the name of the well Esek which means "they argued over it" and moved on to dig another well. But the brothers jocked 'em again. He called that well Sitnah, meaning "accusation," and moving forward, dug yet another well and no one argued over it, so he called it Rehoboth because now they knew that the Almighty had given them a well that was theirs.

And the Almighty appeared to Isaac and told him, "I am the God of your father Abraham. Don't be afraid, 'cuz I'm with you. I will bless you and multiply your kinfolks for My homeboy, Abraham."

Isaac built an altar there and called on the Almighty. He also pitched his tent and let his servant dig a well. And later King Abimelech came to Isaac in Gerar with Ahuzzath, one of his friends, and Phicol, commander of the king's army.

"So, what's up with you?" asked Isaac. "After all you jocked me and sent me away." But the king said that they had seen the works of the Almighty and that he came in peace. "Let's swear to one another and make a deal. You won't jock us and we won't jock you, and we've sent you away in peace and let's keep it that way. You've been blessed, man, by the Almighty."

So it was on and Isaac cooked up a feast and they partied, and then in the morning made the vow to one another, and King Abimelech left with his homeboys in peace.

And later the servants of Isaac told him that they had found water, and they called the well Shebah. The name of the city is Beersheba to this day.

Jacob Steals a Blessing

When Isaac was old and he didn't see so hot, he called his oldest boy Esau to his bedside.

"Here I am, Dad," said Esau.

And Isaac implored his son to take his weapons and get some meat for him to eat before he died and that he would bless him well before he died.

Now Rebekah heard this and when her son Esau went into the field, she went to her son Jacob and told him what she heard. "Now your dad asked Esau to bring him something from the fields so that he could eat it and bless him and die. But I want you to do as I say. Go and get me two good-looking young goats and I will make up a dish your father loves. You can take it to your dad so that he can eat it and the blessing will be yours before he dies."

But Jacob was doubtful. "Look, Ma, I'm sure you realize that Esau is a hairy man and I'm, well, hairless. Perhaps Dad will feel me and know that I'm trying to run a game on him. Then he'll curse me instead of blessing me. No way!"

But his mother was ahead of him. "Let any curse be on me; just do as I say. I know what I'm doing."

And Jacob went and did as his mother said. His mother hit the pots and cooked up a righteous dinner like her husband liked. And she took the good threads from Esau's closet and put them on Jacob, her younger son. And then she wrapped the skins of the goats on his hands and on the smooth part of his neck. And giving him the food, she had Jacob go visit his dad.

"Hey, Dad," said Jacob posing as Esau.

"Who's there?" asked Isaac.

"It's Esau, your first born. I've fixed things like you said, Dad."

But Isaac was doubtful. "How can you have done this so quickly, boy?"

"'Cuz the Almighty brought it to me."

So Isaac said to Jacob, "Please come near so I can feel you. You might not be Esau."

Jacob sat as close as he dared to his father and Isaac felt on him and said, "You sound like Jacob, but the hands are Esau's." He didn't recognize him, but he blessed him. Afterwards he asked, "Are you really my son, Esau?" And Jacob said, "Yeah, Dad."

So Isaac had him come over again to feed him. Jacob fed him and gave him wine to drink. Then Isaac said to him, "Come and kiss me, my son." And Jacob came near again, and Isaac smelled the smell of his clothing and blessed him, saying:

> "Surely, the smell of my son is like the smell of the earth which the Almighty has blessed. So, may God give you all the dew of heaven, the fatness of the earth, and loads of grain and wine. Let brothers serve you, and nations bow down to you. You'll be master over your brothers, and your mother's sons will bow down to you. Curses on anyone who curses you and blessings on all those who bless you."

Then it happened that as soon as Jacob left, and Isaac had finished blessing Jacob, Esau came in from hunting and fixing up his dad's favorite gifts. "Hey, Dad. Come on and eat the meat I've brought and bless me."

"What's going on?" asked Isaac. "Who are you?"

And Esau told him, "I'm your oldest kid, Dad."

And it turned Isaac off for a minute and he cried, "Who? Where is the one who brought me hunted game and fed me. I've blessed him—and you gotta know—that blessing will stick."

When Esau heard his father, he was furious. "Come on, Dad. Bless me, too! You've got to bless me, too!"

And Isaac was sad. "Your brother got one over on me and I've given him your blessing."

And Esau said, "But isn't that just like Jacob? He's gotten over on me twice. First he takes my heritage and now my blessing. Haven't you saved a blessing for me?"

"Yeah," said Isaac, "but I've made him your master. And all brothers I've given him as servants. Grain and wine I have also given him. What can I do now for you, my son?"

> And Esau cried, "Have you only one blessing? Bless me. Even me." And he cried. So Isaac said, "Behold, by your sword you will live, and will serve your brother. And when you've had enough and become restless, you will break the bonds from your neck."

So Esau hated his brother Jacob because of their dad's blessing. Esau promised that when Isaac died, as soon as the days of mourning were over, he was wasting Jacob under no uncertain terms.

But their mother Rebekah called Jacob and said to him. "Look, son. Your brother is just waiting until he can kill you. You gotta get outta here."

And Rebekah sent Jacob to live with her brother Laban in Haran. "Stay there until your brother cools off, and he forgets what you have done to him."

Then Rebekah goes to Isaac and says, "I'm tired of my life here. Suppose Jacob gets some girl from here in Heth. It'll be the end of me if he does."

Jacob Leaves Home

So Isaac called Jacob and blessed him, but admonished him, "Don't get with any of these sisters from Canaan. Go to Padan Aram, to your mother's father hometown and get a sister who is related to Laban, your mother's brother.

> "May God Almighty bless you, and make you fruitful and give you many descendants that you may assemble the people. And you shall have the blessings promised to my father, Abraham, to you and yours, so that you'll inherit that land where you are a foreigner for now, which God gave to Abraham."

And Isaac sent Jacob away and he left for Padan Aram, to Laban, his mother's brother who was the son of Bethuel, the Syrian.

Esau saw that Isaac had blessed Jacob and sent him away to Padan Aram to find him a homegirl for a wife, and Isaac had let Jacob know that he wasn't to marry any girl from Canaan, and also that Jacob did as he was told, and left for Padan Aram. So Esau went over to Ishmael, Abraham's other son, and married the sister of Nebajoth in addition to the wives he already had.

Now Jacob left Beersheba and went to Haran. When he came to a certain place, he lay down for the night since the sun was going down. He took a stone of that place and put it at his head so that he could sleep. And he dreamed.

In the dream a ladder was set on the ground and its top reached to heaven. And the angels were going up and down it. The Almighty stood at the top and said, "I'm the Lord God of Abraham and the God of Isaac. I'm going to give you the very land you sleep on." And the Almighty added: "Your heirs will be like dust and blow across the earth, east to west and north to south, and in you and in your seed all the families of the earth will be blessed." And He charged that he would always be with him wherever Jacob went and one day Jacob would return to that land 'cuz "I'm not going to leave you until I've done what I said I would."

And even though Jacob knew that the Almighty had been in that place, the next morning he was afraid. He felt that the place was actually the house of God and the gateway to heaven. And he called the name of the place Bethel after he had used his rock pillow to make a pillar and poured oil on it.

Then Jacob vowed that as long as the Almighty was with him, and kept him going the right way, and fed him and gave him clothes to wear, he would go back to his father's house in peace and the Almighty shall be his God.

And the stone which Jacob laid for a pillar shall be the Almighty's house and "all that is given to me, I'll return ten percent to You."

The Trials of Jacob

So Jacob went on his way and came upon a group of people from the east. And looking out he saw three flocks of sheep lying by a well which watered the flocks. A big stone was on top of the well covering the opening.

Now when it was time to water the sheep, they would roll off the stone. Jacob asked them where they were from, and they told him, "Haran." So he asked if they knew his uncle Laban, the son of Nahor. And they said, "Yeah, we know him."

"And is he well?"

"Yeah, he is well, and look, his daughter Rachel is coming with the sheep."

And Jacob said, "But it's still rather early. It is not time for the cattle to be rounded up, so water the sheep and go and feed them."

But they could not until all the flocks were together, and then they would roll the stone away. The sheep could then be watered. But when Rachel came near the well, Jacob rolled the stone from the well's mouth and watered the flock of his uncle Laban. And he kissed Rachel and told her that he was Laban's nephew and Rebekah's son. So Laban went down to meet with him and brought him home with him.

"Look, you're my blood," said Laban. "Stay." And Jacob stayed a month.

Now Jacob helped around the house, and his uncle didn't want him working for nothing. "A man gotta get paid," his uncle told him. "What can I give you?"

Laban had two daughters; the name of the oldest was Leah, and then of course there was Rachel who was younger. Leah's eyes were delicate, but Rachel was so fine. Now Jacob loved Rachel and told his uncle, "Look, Uncle, I'll work for seven years for Rachel."

And Laban said, "Okay, man. It's better that she be with you than be given to another man. Stay."

So Jacob served seven years for Rachel and it seemed that they were but a few days away from getting hitched and Jacob was ready. "Give her to me, man. I'm ready."

And a feast was made happenin' and all the brothers of Laban's household came together. But Laban pulled a switch and gave Leah to Jacob and Jacob laid with her. Later, Leah was given a maid named Zilpah from her father.

The next morning when Jacob saw Leah, he went to his uncle. "What's this? You dissing me?   I worked for Rachel and now you deceive me."

And Laban said, "Listen, man. I just couldn't break with tradition. You know the oldest girl got to get married first. Sorry. Look, handle her for the week like tradition says, and I will give you Rachel for say, another seven years."

So Jacob was down for the week and Laban also gave Jacob Rachel. He gave Bilhah to Rachel as a servant.

And Jacob's nose was opened for Rachel and he loved her more. He was down with her as often as possible, but the Almighty saw that Leah was unloved and he let her have a baby with Jacob while with Rachel he did not.

And Leah had a baby boy and named him Reuben, 'cuz she thought, "Now my ol' man will love me."

She had another baby, a son, and named him Simeon because the Almighty knew that she was still unloved.

And when she had a third child, she named him Levi, because she said, "Surely my ol' man will love me now!"

After having a fourth child for Jacob she praised the Almighty and she stopped having kids.

Family Matters

Now Rachel saw that Leah was having kids and she wasn't; she was filled with jealously. She begged her husband to give her a child, but Jacob blew her off. "Do I look like the Almighty? I'm withholding nothing from you, girl." So Rachel gave Jacob her maid Bilhah to have a child for her and Jacob slept with her and had a son with her.

And Rachel felt that God had heard her and given her a son through Bilhah and she called him Dan. And Rachel's maid Bilhah had another son and Rachel thought she was tough. "I've come on the one with my sister," she thought, and she called the boy's name Naphtali.

When Leah saw that she wasn't having any more children, she took Zilpah her maid and gave her to Jacob as wife. And Zilpah had a son who they named Gad because it means "luck." And Leah's maid Zilpah had another son, and they called him Asher.

Now Jacob's son Reuben went around during the wheat harvest and found mandrakes in the field. He took the mandrakes to his mother Leah and when Rachel saw the mandrakes, she asked for some. And Leah said, "What, you take my husband and now you want my son's mandrakes?"

And Rachel told her sister that she could have Jacob that night for the mandrakes, so that when Jacob came home, Leah told him, "You gotta stay with me, for I have paid for my time with you with my son's mandrakes." So he did and Leah conceived that night and gave Jacob a fifth son. And she called him Issachar, because God had given her due. And Leah conceived yet again and gave

Jacob a sixth son, and named him Zebulun because the Almighty was truly blessing her.

Later she had a daughter whose name was Dinah.

But God had not forgotten Rachel and later she did get pregnant and had a son whom she called Joseph. "Now God has taken the bad luck from me."

And when Rachel had Joseph, Jacob went to his uncle Laban and asked to be sent away "to go hang out in my own place and my own country." He asked for his wives and children because he had done plenty for Laban.

But Laban didn't want him to go. "Stay, brother. You've blessed me so much. Stay and name your price."

But Jacob didn't want to stay. He felt that he had increased Laban's wealth and was ready. But Laban implored him. "What can I give you?"

"Nothing, man. Look I'll feed and care for your flock today, and let me remove all the speckled and spotted sheep and the brown ones from the lambs, and the spotted and speckled from the goats, and this shall be payment enough."

"And, look," said Jacob. "If you find any that isn't speckled or spotted you can consider it stolen. "Okay?"

And Laban said, "Okay."

But that day he removed the goats that were speckled and spotted, male and female, and all the little brown lambs, too—all which were to have been Jacob's.

And he put some distance between he and Jacob, and Jacob fed the rest of his uncle's flock.

Now Jacob took rods of green poplar and of the almond and chestnut trees, peeled white strips in them and exposed the white in the rods. And the rods he set before the flocks in the gutters where they took their water, so that they would get pregnant when they drank.

And the flocks conceived before the rods and had speckled and spotted lambs. Then Jacob separated the lambs and placed them facing the streaked and he put his own flocks by themselves so that they wouldn't be with Laban's flock.

And when they were fertile, Jacob placed the rod before their eyes, and when the flocks were feeble, he did not. And so Jacob had the stronger flock and the weaker ones belonged to Laban.

And Jacob became rich beyond belief. He had large flocks, female and male servants, as well as camels and donkeys.

Jacob Flees His Uncle's Crib

Now Jacob heard the gossip coming from Laban's sons who said, "Jacob has been jocking our dad and taken what is his. He's gotten wealthy off our dad." And Jacob became hip to the fact that Laban felt somewhat the same way.

And the Almighty gave charge that Jacob should leave his uncle's land and return to his father's place.

And Jacob told Leah and Rachel that he was leaving 'cuz he didn't think their father was too happy anyway and was waiting on a chance to take care of him. And he told them that he had been fair with their father, but that their father hadn't been on the up and up even in the beginning.

"Look, ladies. The speckled flocks were to be my wages and they grew strong. But no, now your father is jocking me again and I'm tired of it. And even the Almighty sees what your father is doing to me and has asked me to leave here."

So Rachel and Leah answered and said to him, "Is there anything of our father that belongs to us? We're practically strangers to him, for he sold us and also completely consumed our dough. Look, everything that was taken from our father and given to you was ours anyways. Now do whatever God has told you. We're square with it."

So Jacob took his family and set them upon camels to drive themselves out of Laban's home town. And he took his flock and possessions, but Rachel stole the household idols that were her father's.

And like a thief in the night, Jacob took off without Laban's knowledge or permission. He headed towards the mountains of Gilead.

On the third day, Laban became aware that Jacob was gone. And he got his homeboys together to take after them. But in the middle of the night the Almighty came to Laban in a dream and warned him, "Be careful how you speak 'bout my boy, Jacob."

So Laban caught up with Jacob and admonished him for leaving so secretly. "What's with you, man? You steal away in the middle of the night, take my daughters and then steal from my house. Why did you do this? I'd have let you go. Really. You didn't even let me kiss my grandkids good-bye."

"Look," he added, "I could really jock you for this, but your God said for me to watch my step."

And Jacob answered, "Okay, man. I was afraid. I thought that maybe you would take my ol' ladies away from me. But as for stealing from you, man, if you find anything that belongs to you, you can have it. And let death be on whoever did steal from you." But Jacob didn't know that his wife Rachel had copped the idols.

Laban looked in Leah's tent, the servants' tents, the two maids, but he did not find them. Then he went to Rachel's tent, but Rachel had taken the household idols and put them in the camel's saddle and sat on them. And Laban searched and searched but did not find them.

And she told her father that she couldn't rise to meet him since it was that time of the month. Because of this Laban didn't find the idols.

So now Jacob was miffed and told Laban, "What is this, man? You accuse me of taking your things. You've searched everywhere. It's an embarrassment, man. An insult!

"I've been with you more than twenty years—taken more stuff off you than the law allows. You don't know how this galls me.

"When animals were taken by wild beasts, I didn't even bring them to you to show you it wasn't my fault. And you even made me pay for anything stolen, day or night. No matter what, you could depend on me. And if the Almighty had not been with me, it's no telling what else you would have done to me. Even God has seen what you have done and He let you know it, too!"

Laban answered, "Look, Jacob, these are my daughters! These are my children, and this flock is my flock. All that you see is mine. What do you think I'd do to these women and their children? Come on, let's make a deal we can all live with."

So Jacob took a stone and set it up as a pillar and Jacob told his homeboys to gather more stones. And they made the stones into piles, then sat down to eat. Jacob named the place and Laban agreed that it should be called Galeed ("'cuz this heap is a witness between us"). It was also called Mizpah because Laban asked the Almighty to "Watch between us, man, when we're apart." Laban went on to say, "If you mess over my daughters or take on another woman, God'll know." And as a symbol of all that was said, Laban looked at the pile of rocks and said, "This pile bears witness we won't cross these piles of rocks to hurt each other."

Jacob agreed and swore on his daddy's grave that he would. He offered a sacrifice on the mountain and broke bread with his brothers. They all broke bread together and stayed 'round the mountain 'til morning.

The next day, Laban got up early, kissed his grandkids and his daughters and blessed them. Then he went home.

Homeward Bound

Jacob left Laban's land and the angels of God met him along the way. When Jacob saw them he said, "This is God's base." And the name of the place was called Mahanaim. Then Jacob sent messengers to his brother Esau. His message was, "I've been to Laban's land and stayed until now. I have oxen, donkeys, flocks, and male and female servants; and now I'm asking for leniency."

Then the messengers returned to Jacob and said, "Your brother is coming to meet you. He's got four hundred brothers with him."

And Jacob was real scared and he divided the people that were with him. "Look, if Esau attacks one or the other, the others can escape." He set out to pray.

And Jacob asked the Almighty, "Look, I know I'm not worth all this, but I'm asking that you show mercy. Deliver me from the wrath of my brother, Esau, 'cuz I'm scared for me and my family. Lord, you've promised me to treat me well, and I'm asking only that you remember."

And Jacob spent the night and gathered a present for his brother which consisted of two hundred female goats, twenty male goats, two hundred ewes and twenty rams, thirty milk camels with their colts, forty cows and ten bulls, twenty female donkeys and ten foals.

And he gave this to one of his homeboys to give to his brother Esau. "And when Esau asks who these belong to, you will tell him that they are his—a present from his little brother, Jacob."

And he told each of his servants to say this when and if they saw Esau. And they were to each let Esau know that Jacob was behind him.

So they went and did as they were told. Jacob meantime took his wives, his maidservants and his eleven sons and crossed over the Jabbok River to safety. The family went over the brook while Jacob stayed alone.

And that night a man wrestled with Jacob until the breaking of day. Now when He saw that He couldn't beat up Jacob and win, He touched the socket of Jacob's hip and moved it out of joint.

Even though his hip was out of joint, Jacob held on.

And the man said, "Let me go, man. It's almost daytime," but Jacob wouldn't let go.

"Not 'til you bless me!"

"What's your name?"

"Jacob."

"Okay. Your name is no longer Jacob. It'll now be Israel 'cuz you wrestled with both God and man, and came out on top."

And Jacob asked the name of Him, who wanted to know, "What for, man?"

Jacob was blessed there in that place and called it Peniel 'cuz he'd seen the face of God and lived to tell 'bout it.

He then limped on as the sun rose. And the kids of Israel never eat the muscle that shrank on the hip socket, because the Almighty touched Jacob's hip there.

Making Up for Lost Time

Now Jacob looked up and coming 'round the bend was Esau with four hundred men. So he told part of his children to go with Leah, part with Rachel, and the rest with maidservants. He put the servants first with their children, then Leah and her children and last he placed Rachel and Joseph. And he came before Esau and bowed to the ground seven times as he approached his brother.

But Esau ran to meet him and hugged him tight, weeping and kissing his neck. And when he looked up, he noticed the women and children.

"Who are they?" he asked.

And Abraham answered, "My kids and family who the Almighty blessed me with."

And the family came up and bowed; Leah and her children, Rachel and her kids.

And Esau asked, "What's up?" To which Jacob begged Esau to accept his gifts, but Esau refused.

"I have enough," said Esau. "You don't have to buy me. Come on and join me."

But Jacob begged off for a moment saying that the family was tired from the journey. "They're weak. We'll catch up with you."

"Well, let me leave some of my people here for you," said Esau, "so you won't have to rush." Then he asked, "What else can I do for you? I want you to like me."

And Jacob went to Succoth and took up residence. Later he went to the city of Shechem, which is in the land of Canaan, and he decided to live there. Then he bought that land for one hundred pieces of money.

He put up an altar and called the place El Elohe Israel, or "El, God of Israel."

The Rape of Dinah

Now Leah's daughter, Dinah, who was also Jacob's daughter, went outside to scope things out. And when Shechem, the son of Hamor the Hivite and prince of the country, saw her, he raped her. He thought Dinah was so fine and he was so attracted to her that he was real nice to her afterwards.

Then Shechem asked his dad to get him this woman for his ol' lady, but Jacob hearing that he had raped his daughter was angry. Shechem's father came to Jacob and said, "Look, I know that this is not good what Shechem has done, but he's really turned on by your daughter. Let 'em get married. It's the best thing for both of them."

And Shechem said, "Look, what can I do to get in your graces? Tell me how much and that will be alright with me."

But Jacob didn't want to do this and neither did his sons. It just wasn't cool. "Look, we can't do this, but on one condition. You must circumcise yourselves as we are. That way you can marry my daughter, but if you don't then I have no choice but to take my daughter away from here."

And it was right-on with Hamor and Shechem, his son. And Shechem did this as soon as possible because he really loved that woman.

"Look, there's plenty of room for all of us. And we can do this, work and live together. It'll work."

And so every man was circumcised.

But Jacob's sons, Simeon and Levi, Dinah's brothers, were not satisfied, so on the third day, they wasted Hamor and Shechem with a sword. Then Dinah's other brothers went to the Shechem's city and killed all the men and took their things. They took sheep, oxen, and donkeys, and all that was in the city and what was in the field—all their money.

And Jacob was fighting mad at his boys. "This is a very bad thing you have done," he said. "Now they will rise and kill us. You stupid..."

But the sons said, "So, we should let them treat our sister like a whore?"

Death of Rachel and Isaac

The Almighty told Jacob to "Get up and go into Bethel and live there." And He charged Jacob to make an altar to

Him who showed up when he was scared of his brother Esau.

And Jacob got his family together again, and said, "No more false gods. Clean yourselves up and change your clothes."

He told them of going to Bethel because the Almighty had told them to and because the Almighty had been good to them. So everyone got rid of everything that was godless—all their earrings which were in their ears; and Jacob hid them under a tree by Shechem.

And they left and God's Spirit sent terror to all those cities and no one touched Jacob. So when Jacob came to Luz (that is, Bethel), which is in the land of Canaan, he and all his family were still with him. And he built an altar like he was told and called it El Bethel because God appeared to him when he ran away from his brother.

Now Deborah, Rebekah's nurse died and she was buried under the terebinth tree in Bethel.

Then God appeared to Jacob one more time, and blessed him. And the Almighty said, "Your name is Jacob now, but in the future you shall be called Israel." So Jacob called himself Israel.

Also, the Almighty told him, "I am God Almighty. Be fruitful and multiply. Nations will come from your blood, as will royalty."

And the Almighty promised that the land which was given to Abraham and Isaac was now given to him. So as the Almighty talked with Jacob, now Israel, he set up a pillar and poured oil on it as was the custom and Jacob called the place where the Almighty spoke Bethel.

When Jacob came back, he was told that Rachel was in labor with their child. And the midwife told her to "be calm. Nothing going to happen to this child." But Rachel died while in labor, though not before her son was born and she had named him Ben-Oni. Jacob, however, called him Benjamin.

And Rachel was buried on the way to Bethlehem. And Jacob put a marker on her grave which is still there to this day. And while he was away burying his wife, Reuben went and slept with Bilhah, Jacob's concubine; and Jacob heard about it and was furious.

Now Jacob had twelve sons[15] and his brother Esau had many descendants as well.[16] After Rachel died, Jacob took his sons to be with his dad, Isaac, before he died. Isaac had lived to be one hundred and eight years of age. Esau and Jacob buried him together, as brothers.

Joseph's Dreams Get Him Into Trouble

Now Jacob lived in the land where his father had been a stranger: the land of Canaan. His son Joseph, who was seventeen, fed the flock with his brothers.[17] Joseph, it seems, was a tattletale and his brothers were plenty upset about it.

---

[15]See the descendents of Jacob in Genesis, Chapter 35, versus 23 through 26.

[16]The descendents of Esau can be found in Chapter 36 of Genesis.

[17]The story of Joseph is found in Genesis, Chapters 37 through 50.

You see, Joseph was loved by his father more than all his children because he was born when Jacob was old. Jacob made him a jacket of many colors.

And when Jacob's sons saw that he loved Joseph more, they got bent out of shape. They hated Joseph, especially since they thought him such a brat. So when he started having dreams and told them those dreams, they were really peeved. And here is one of Joseph's dreams:

> "Man, there we were binding sheaves in the field. Then guess what? My sheaf rose and stood upright and your sheaves stood around my sheaf and bowed. Imagine?"

And his brothers said to him, "What? You think we will serve you, you selfish brat? Think again!" The brothers grumbled among themselves then, hating Joseph even more.

Then Joseph dreamed another dream and said to his brothers, "Guess what? I've dreamed something else."

In this dream he told them that the sun, the moon and the eleven stars bowed down to him. "Ain't that a lick?: He also told his father who fussed gently at him. "What is this dreaming stuff, boy? You want us to bow down to you? Get a life," he admonished. "You gotta stop with this dreaming." Still, Israel thought hard about what Joseph was saying.

Later when the brothers went to feed the stock they decided that they had enough of Joseph and his puny dreams, so they were gonna waste him. And when Jacob sent Joseph down to his brothers (not knowing what they wanted to do), the brothers had already hatched a plan.

When Joseph went looking for his brothers they ambushed him.

"Look, here comes the dreamer. Is he ever gonna get it."

But Reuben heard all about it and what all they intended to do. In fact, if it wasn't for Reuben, Joseph would have been wasted right then and there. But using his head, he threw Joseph into a pit somewhere in the wilderness ordering his brothers "not to touch him. Okay? I mean it." Reuben told 'em that this way Joseph's blood would not be on their hands, but he was really planning on saving Joseph later.

But the brothers had other ideas. Before Joseph was thrown into the pit, the brothers ripped Joseph's tunic off his body. And then they grabbed some grub. And while they were eating, they saw some guys from the Ishmaelites (traders who sold spices, balm and myrrh) who were on their way to Egypt.

So Judah said, "Look, let's not kill Joseph. Let's sell him!"

And the brothers agreed, "Yeah, get the brat outta the city."

So the brothers pulled Joseph from the pit and sold him to the Ishmaelites for twenty shekels of silver. The traders took Joseph on down to Egypt with them.

When Reuben went back to the pit, Joseph was gone. His brothers simply told him, "He's outta here, man." And Reuben didn't know what his brothers had done and he was really scared.

The brothers, though, had to think fast. So to make their plan work, they took Joseph's coat and killed a goat kid and dipped the coat in it so that it would look like some wild beast had eaten the boy. They took it to Jacob who knew that the coat belonged to Joseph saying, "A wild beast has gotten hold of the boy. Poor Joseph had been torn to pieces."

And Jacob was devastated. He tore his clothes, put on sackcloth, and cried for many days. His sons and daughters tried to comfort him, but he wouldn't have it. He loved Joseph so much.

Meanwhile, Joseph was sold to Potiphar, an officer of Pharaoh and captain of the guard.

The Story of Judah

Judah left his brothers' and his father's house and moved to Adullam. There Judah fell for a fine daughter of a Canaanite whose name was Shua and he married her. She got pregnant and had a son called Er.

Then she got pregnant again and had a son named Onan. And then she got pregnant again and had a son named Shelah.

Judah got a wife for his oldest boy, Er, and her name was Tamar. But Er was one bad dude and the Almighty blew him away. And Judah said to his son Onan, "Look, go to your brother's wife, marry her, and sleep with her. This way your dead brother can have an heir."

But Onan knew that the child would legally not be his and so when he slept with Tamar, he only pretended to get with her and his sperm went on the ground so that she wouldn't get pregnant. And the Almighty was not pleased, so he blew Onan away, too.

Then Judah said to Tamar, "Look, stay a widow until my son Shelah is grown." And she lived with Judah. But

Judah was afraid that Shelah would be killed (just in case he didn't mind the Almighty either), so he wasn't about to hand Shelah over to sleep with Tamar. He didn't want this son dying as well.

During this period, Judah's wife died. His homeboy, Hirah the Adullamite, comforted him and tried to make him feel better where they shear sheep. And someone told Tamar that her father-in-law was headed that way, so she broke out of her widow's clothes and covered her face with a veil and dressed up for the occasion.

See, Tamar could see that Shelah was all grown up and Judah was gonna break his promise to her. She knew that she was not going to be his wife or anybody else's for that matter, so she decided to take matters into her own hands.

Well, she was all dressed up and sitting on the side of the road when Judah saw who he thought to be a common whore. And being sad and all, with needs of his own, he asked her to be down with him, and she agreed on the condition that he pledge something valuable. "I ain't doing this for free," she said. And when he asked what she wanted she answered, "Your ring and chain, and also the cane you carry." So, it was agreed and Tamar and Judah got busy and she became pregnant.

Afterwards, Tamar dressed again like the widow and went home. Now in the meantime, Judah had a chance to think things over and so he had his friend, the Adullamite, go and get his things back. "I can't be leaving my things with no whore," he begged. But when they got there, the sister he thought was a whore was nowhere to be found. It was as if she had vanished into thin air. In fact, Judah's friend thought he was a little touched in the head to have dreamed up some woman sitting on the side of the road.

"Hey man, it's alright. I know how bothered you've been these last few days, what with your ol' lady dying and all. Don't worry about it."

But to be sure, he asked around. "Where's that whore who was sitting on the side of the road?" And no one knew what he was talking about. So, he went back to his friend, Judah, to tell him that he couldn't find the sister.

Judah answered that it was just as well, since finding her might bring shame on him. "Look, I don't want no problems. Leave it alone."

After a few months had gone by, people started talking about his daughter-in-law and how she was in the family way.

"Hey, brother. Your daughter-in-law ain't all this and that. The girl has gone and gotten herself pregnant. And she ain't even married no more."

"The girl's a whore," said others.

So Judah said, "Bring her here. If she's been messing around, especially while living in my crib, we'll just have to burn her at the stake. I can't be having her dissing me in my own house."

And when Tamar was brought around, she said, "Yeah, it's true I'm pregnant, but look, I'll tell you who the father is." And pulling out some things from her bag, she said, "He's the one who owns this ring and chain as well as this cane."

And Judah was shocked, but what could he do? He knew that he was the one who had really dissed the sister by not letting her marry his baby boy, so Judah 'fessed up to having slept with the girl and took responsibility for the child, but he never got busy with her again.

Tamar was pregnant with twins and when it was time to deliver, the first child put out his hand and the midwife tied a red string 'round it. But the child drew his hand back in, and the second child came through instead, so they named him Perez because it means "breakthrough." And the child with the thread around his hand was called Zerah.

The Trials of Joseph

Joseph had been taken down to Egypt where Potiphar, an officer of Pharaoh, captain of the guard, and also an Egyptian, bought him from the Ishmaelites who had made him a slave. And the Almighty was riding Joseph well, 'cuz he didn't leave him even for a minute. And Joseph was in good stead with the Almighty so that soon the masters of Joseph made him an overseer (a person who takes care of things for the master).

The Egyptians were blessed having Joseph around. And Joseph was given much responsibility. So much responsibility, in fact, that Joseph was in total control.

Joseph was good-looking. He was one fine and well built brother. And the boss's wife noticed it. Everywhere Joseph went, she was somewhere around, smacking her lips.

"Let's get busy," she begged. "You don't know how you really turn me on." But Joseph couldn't betray a homeboy that way. Also, he couldn't jock the Almighty either, 'cuz it wouldn't be right sleeping with somebody else's ol' lady. He told the woman "no."

And the homegirl was really peeved, but she wasn't giving up, no matter what.

One day the homegirl got her chance to be alone with Joseph, and she pulled herself up on him, and begged him to sleep with her. "Come on Joseph. How can you turn this down? Ain't I fine?" And lookin' him up and down, she said, "What's a girl gotta do to get with you?"

But Joseph wasn't having it, so he got as far away from her as he could.

But hell hath no fury like a woman scorned, and the homegirl set Joseph up, saying to the other servants, "Look at what my husband has brought into my house. This man is a Hebrew and tried to rape me."

And she repeated the story to her husband who was furious that Joseph had betrayed him this way, although he hadn't. So they threw the homeboy into jail for a crime he didn't commit. But all in all, the Almighty stood by Joseph, 'cuz *He knew* that Joseph hadn't done the wild thing, and the guards in prison liked him too and were easy on him.

In fact, the guards didn't even jock Joseph while in prison. They trusted him to watch over and help with the other prisoners. And all this happened 'cuz the Almighty was in Joseph's corner.

The Telling of Dreams

The butler and baker of the King of Egypt fell into disfavor and the Pharaoh sent the homeboys to jail. And these two were put in the custody of Joseph who was still in jail (for the lie Potiphar's wife told). While in the prison, the butler and baker both had dreams that troubled them. It really worried their heads.

The next morning Joseph noticed that the two prisoners were bent out of shape over something, so he asked, "What's up, fellows?" And they told him.

"We've had nightmares, each of us and there's nothin' funny about 'em. There's no one to tell us what they mean. If they're gonna worry us, we outta know what they mean."

And Joseph told them that interpretations of dreams belonged to the Almighty and asked them to tell him about their dreams. So the butler said:

> "Well, in my dream a vine was in front of me and the vine had three branches. It was as if the vines blossomed and it made beautiful grapes. Then Pharaoh's cup was in my hand and I took those grapes and mashed them and placed the cup in Pharaoh's hand."

Joseph said, "This is what it means. The tree branches are three days. Now in three days Pharaoh will forgive you and give you back your old gig. And you will put Pharaoh's cup in his hand just like you did when you were the butler before." And then Joseph made the butler promise that when things were righteous for him, "You won't forget me, man."

And Joseph felt comfortable with the butler and laid out his life story. He told the butler how he was stolen from his family and didn't really belong in jail, especially since he hadn't done anything.

When the baker saw that the butler's dream didn't seem so bad, he told Joseph his dream:

> "In my dream were three white baskets on my head. There were all kinds of baked goods for the Pharaoh, but the birds ate them out of the baskets on my head."

And Joseph said, "This is the meaning. The three baskets are three days and within those three days Pharaoh will hang you on a tree and the birds will eat your flesh. Hey, man, I'm really sorry."

Now the third day was Pharaoh's birthday and he gave the butler back his job and hung the baker. But the butler was so happy to get his gig back, he forgot all about telling the Pharaoh of Joseph.

Seven Years a Plenty, Seven Years a Wasted

Two years passed and Joseph was still locked up. And it happened that the Pharaoh had his own nightmares and they shook him up pretty bad. And Pharaoh's dream was:

> "Pharaoh was standing by a river and suddenly came from the river seven really nice looking cows; fine and fat and they ate in the meadows. But later seven other cows which were ugly and skinny stood by the other cows and ate up the fat, fine cows."

And Pharaoh would wake up in a cold sweat. And then he dreamed again. And this was Pharaoh's dream:

> Seven heads of grain came up on one stalk,
> plump and good, and then seven thin heads
> from the east came up after the good ones. And
> the seven thin heads ate the seven plump ones."

Pharaoh was scared. He sent for the wise men of his country, but they couldn't tell him what his dreams meant. In fact, it looked like no one could help the brother out. There was simply no one.

But then the butler remembered Joseph and told Pharaoh, "Look, maybe I'm speaking outta turn, but there's this guy who told me what my dreams meant and he's good." And then the butler told him about the dreams that he and the homeboy baker had and how he had come back to serve Pharaoh and, well, they hung home dude, just like Joseph said. "I think you ought give him a call."

So Pharaoh sent for Joseph.

"Look, man, I hear tell you can decipher dreams."

And Joseph answered Pharaoh, saying, "It ain't me, sir. The Almighty will give you an answer to your dreams."

So Pharaoh told Joseph the dream. "I was standing by a river and suddenly came from the river seven really nice-looking cows; fine and fat and they ate in the meadows. But later seven other cows which were ugly and skinny stood by the other cows and ate up the fat, fine cows. And I dreamed again. Seven heads of grain came up on one stalk, plump and good and then seven thin heads from the east came up after the good ones. And the seven thin heads ate the seven plump ones."

And Joseph said, "The dreams are one and the same. This is the meaning of your dreams. You see, the first seven cows are seven good years. And the same with the heads of grain. God is showing you a sign, sir.

"This town will have seven good years where there'll be plenty for everyone. And the seven terrible cows and sad heads of grains stand for a time when a famine will dry up these fields to a crisp. Now here's what you ought to do:

"You need someone to kinda run things during the time of plenty. He can take part of the things produced in the first year and bank it. Then when the bad times come, you'll have enough banked to survive the rough times."

Now Pharaoh really thought this interpretation was right-on. He could see that the dream meant exactly as Joseph had said, and so Pharaoh asked his servants, "Look, who could do this job?"

And they didn't know 'cuz they didn't know much. After all, it was Joseph was told Pharaoh what the dream meant.

So to Joseph he said, "I think you can, man. After all, if you could see the dream for what it is when no one else could, well that clinches it for me. You got the job. I won't take no for an answer."

Pharaoh then took off his signet ring and put it on Joseph's hand. And he put on him some of the finest threads as well as a gold chain around his neck. And Joseph rode in a chariot right next to the Pharaoh so that folks bowed to him just like they did to Pharaoh.

Joseph's name was then changed to Zaphnath-Paaneah by Pharaoh, who also gave Joseph a fine ol' lady named Asenath, the daughter of Poti-Pherah, a priest of On. And the homeboy was only thirty years old when all this went down.

The seven years of plenty came and went, and Joseph banked the extra food to prepare for the lean years. And Joseph worked his gig, had two sons which the daughter of Poti-Pherah the priest bore, Manasseh (the eldest, whose name means "God has made me forget how rough things have been") and Ephraim (the baby boy, whose name means "God has made me fruitful").

And then the hard times came and people went crying to Pharaoh. But Pharaoh sent them to Joseph, telling them, "Whatever he says is cool."

So, all countries came to Joseph to buy grain because times were really rough.

Joseph's Brothers Get What's Coming

Jacob saw that there was grain in Egypt and he asked his sons to go there. "What's wrong with you guys?" he asked. "Why are you looking at one another like that?"

And Jacob said, "It's true. There's grain in Egypt. Go down and buy for us so that we can live and not die."

So Joseph's brothers went down to buy grain in Egypt. But Jacob kept his son Benjamin home with him, "so that nothing will happen to my boy."

And the sons of Israel went to buy grain along with those who were also looking for grain.

Now Joseph was governor over the land and he sold to all the brothers and sisters everywhere. And Joseph's brothers came and bowed down before him and Joseph recognized them, but jocked 'em and pretended he didn't. And he spoke roughly to him.

"Where you from?" he asked harshly.

"The Land of Canaan," they replied because they didn't recognize him.

"Well, I think you're spies. You have come to see if we're all 'bout this and that."

"We are one man's sons, man. We don't want to jock you. No sir!"

But Joseph wasn't buying it. "You're spies, I tell you." And he looked like he was gonna throw 'em all in jail right there on the spot.

But then he softened a bit. "But I tell you what. Bring me your youngest brother, Benjamin, and if you're telling the truth you will live. I'll keep one of your brothers here with me. If you lie...he dies!"

The brothers were feeling guilty. If only they hadn't done evil to their other brother, Joseph. If only they could turn back the hands of time. They told their oldest brother, Reuben, what they had really done.

"Hey, man. We're sorry. This curse is on our heads 'cuz we wouldn't leave that boy alone."

And Reuben said, "I knew it! I told you guys not to do that, and you went ahead and did this. What's wrong with you? Why didn't you listen? Now look what his blood on our hands is doing."

And they were a pitiful sight, 'cuz they still did not know that Joseph was their brother for he spoke to them through an interpreter like he didn't understand Hebrew when he really did.

Joseph had to turn his back and wipe the tears from his eyes 'cuz he felt bad, but turning back to them, he pointed to Simeon. "Leave him with me," he ordered and turned away, but not before giving the brothers sacks of grain for provisions.

Later when one of the brothers opened the sacks he found money on top of the grain. He thought that maybe their money was being returned, but they were still afraid. "What's going on, Lord?" they implored. "We can't take this."

Then they went to Jacob, their dad, and told him all that happened. "This man is lord of the land and thought we were spies. Honest, we told him we weren't, but he wasn't buying it. So he asked that we bring our youngest brother to him and by this he would know that we were honest. Dad, he took Simeon."

And when they emptied the sacks of grain they found money in each sack.

"Oh, what have you boys done now?" questioned Jacob. "First I lose Joseph. Now Simeon, and you want me to give you Benjamin. What is happenin' here?"

Then Reuben told his dad, "Look, kill my two sons if I do not bring Benjamin back to you. Put this on my shoulders and I will bring Benjamin back."

"Nah," said the father. "Should anything happen to Benjamin, it'll be my death. He cannot go."

Joseph's Plan

There wasn't nothing to eat for miles around, so when they were finally running out of food, Jacob asked the brothers to go back and buy some food. But Judah warned that they could go not unless that governor could see Benjamin.

"Look, Dad, if you send Benjamin with us, we'll go. But if you will not send him with us, we can't go. The guy won't even show his face unless Benjamin is with us. And, anyway, he's still got Simeon."

And Israel said, "Why did you deal so poorly with this man? What has he got to do with us?"

And it was surely a puzzle. "Yeah. The man even asked if our father was alive. And asking if we had another brother? It's almost as if he could see right into our home. How could we have known that he would ask us to bring Benjamin? What could we do?"

Then Judah said to Israel, his dad, "Look, send the boy with me and we will go down there in order to put food on the table. We don't want to die. If we hadn't stayed so long here, we would be back by now. As it stands, it's gonna be rough either way. We gotta take Ben, Dad. We've got to."

And Jacob, having no choice, said, "Okay. Take some fruit in our best containers and carry down a present for the man: a little balm and a little honey, spices and myrrh, pistachio nuts and almonds. And this time, double the money in your hand. Take back the money he returned 'cuz it was probably a mistake. And take Benjamin and I'll pray that the Almighty will have mercy. I can't lose my baby."

So the brothers did as their father had them do and when they returned to Egypt they took Benjamin and double the money. When Joseph saw Benjamin he asked his servant to "kill an animal for dinner because these men will have supper with me." The man obeyed. Now the brothers were afraid because they were brought into Joseph's house and they knew it was 'cuz of the money. "He's gonna make us slaves," said one.

And when they were brought into Joseph's house, they pleaded, "Look, we really did come to buy grain the time before. We found the money after we left." They were explaining things left and right.

But the servant told them to "Be still." He told them not to be afraid for "Your God and the God of your father has given you everything you have." Then he brought out Simeon.

So the boys were brought into the house and their donkeys were fed. The brothers were told that they would eat supper there.

And when Joseph came home, they gave him presents. Joseph inquired of their father. "Is he in good health? He is still alive, isn't he?"

And they answered yes.

Then lifting his eyes, Joseph saw Benjamin, his brother and his mother's son and said, "Is this your younger brother that you told me about?" And he said to Benjamin, "God be gracious to you, man."

Now Joseph wanted to cry and he excused himself so that he wouldn't get all weepy in front of everyone. And he let them eat because they couldn't eat together. (In those days it was a rule that Egyptians and Hebrews didn't eat together.) But they sat down according to their date of birth, and all were served, but Benjamin was given five times what his brothers were given. In fact, Joseph made sure that Benjamin was treated almost like royalty.

And the brothers partied hearty, 'though they still didn't know Joseph was their brother.

Plan in Effect

So Joseph told his servants to fill the men's sacks with as much food as they could carry. But he also told his servant to put a silver cup in Benjamin's sack.

And he sent his brothers on their way, but as soon as they were out of the city, Joseph asked his steward to "Get up, follow the men; and when you find them, say to them 'Why have you repaid my master with evil after all he's done for you?'

"And look in the bags and find the cup and ask, Wasn't this from my master's house? You thieves!'"

And it was done, but the brothers were appalled. "How could you think such a thing? Didn't we bring back double the money? Look, if you find something then let whoever has it die!"

And so the search was done and the cup was found in Benjamin's sack.

"I didn't take nothing." Benjamin said to his brothers. "I swear." And the brothers had every right to be afraid.

They were taken back to Joseph's house who showed his displeasure with the brothers though he really wasn't mad at all. And Judah said to Joseph, "What can we do about this? I can't believe Ben would do something like this. He didn't do it."

But Joseph wasn't buying it. He said, "Look the brother that had the cup has to be my slave now. The rest of you should to go on home."

"But, please, my lord. He didn't. You don't know Benjamin. He wouldn't do this. Look, don't do this," begged Judah. "What can we say? What can we do?"

But Joseph was adamant. "It's done. You said so yourself. Look, the cup was found in the boy's sack. Now go home to your father."

But Judah would not give up. "Please, sir. Don't be offended, for we know you're as powerful as the big guy, Pharaoh. But wasn't it you who asked about my father and brother? And we told you that we had a father and a much younger brother, as our father had him when he was already old.

"And you wanted to see this young man for yourself, even though bringing him here was surely a hard thing for our dad, but even so we brought him. We had to plead with our father to let him come with us.

"You see, my father lost one child to tragic circumstances, and if he loses this son, he will just die. I know it.

"How can I go to my father if our brother is not with me? Can you really let this happen to our father?"

The Game Is Up

Joseph couldn't keep up the game. He asked that all his servants leave so that he could be alone with his brothers.

And Joseph could not stop himself. He made everyone leave his presence with the exception of his brothers. And he cried because he was so filled with emotion.

"Are you really this dense? Look at me. I am Joseph, your brother. You mean my father is still alive?"

And Joseph walked down to stand face-to-face with his brothers. And these brothers looked like they had just seen a ghost. They couldn't believe what their eyes were telling them.

"Look, don't be angry with yourselves about what you did to me so many years ago. Don't you know that it was the plan of the Almighty all along? We've survived two years of famine, and we've got another five years to go before things get better. You gotta realize that it was the Almighty who sent me here to keep you safe.

"Now here's what I want you to do. Go to my father and let him know that I am alive and running things right here in Egypt. Tell him I don't want him struggling there in Canaan, but you are to live near me in Goshen.

"Tell him I'll take care of him and all of you. I don't want you poor and struggling.

"And if you don't believe it is me, just look at Benjamin, my brother. See the resemblance. The eyes—look at the eyes.

"Now hurry and bring Dad here."

And then Joseph wept with his arms around Benjamin's neck. He kissed each of his brothers and let them know that all was well.

Everyone in Egypt had heard that Joseph's brothers were there in Egypt and all the gossip that went with knowing. Even Pharaoh got wind of it, but urged Joseph to do what he had to do.

"Bring your dad. I'll give your family the best land in town."

And the sons of Israel went to get their dad. And Joseph gave them enough things to travel there and bring back their families. He gave them clothes, too, but to Benjamin he gave three hundred pieces of silver and five changes of garments. To his father he sent ten donkeys loaded with good things of Egypt, and ten female donkeys loaded with grain, bread and food for this journey. And when he sent his brothers away, he told 'em not to get into any trouble.

When the brothers told Jacob that Joseph was alive, he didn't believe them. But the brothers kept on telling him that it was true until finally Jacob believed.

"It's true. Joseph is alive and, get this, running things in Egypt." And Jacob was relieved that he would see his son again before he died.

Israel's Happiness

Israel (Jacob) took off for Egypt, but not before making a sacrifice to God. And the Almighty spoke to Israel in a vision and told him not to be afraid to go to Egypt.

And He explained to Israel that He would be with him in Egypt just as he was in Canaan. And they took everything with them to Egypt. They took their livestock and their goods, everything they had accumulated over the years. Jacob went with his entire family.

And these are the names of the children of Israel:

Jacob and his sons went to Egypt. It was Reuben who was Jacob's firstborn. Reuben's sons went too. In fact, almost everyone in Jacob's hometown went to live with Joseph, his sons and their sons too, so that the family of Jacob lived in Egypt.[18]

---

[18]For a complete look at the family of Jacob (Israel), read Genesis, Chapter 46. Not all of Jacob's family went to Egypt, however.

There were sixty-six people in all who went with Jacob to Egypt. With Joseph and his two sons there were seventy family members in Egypt.

Judah went ahead of the party to find out directions to Goshen. And when they got there, Joseph came in his chariot to greet his father firsthand. And they embraced each other and cried because it had been so long. Israel said to Joseph, "Now I can die in peace, knowing my son is alive."

Joseph promised his brothers that everything would be alright. In fact, Joseph went to Pharaoh to tell him his family was here and that they were shepherds (for this was their gig). He explained to his brothers that when they got to see Pharaoh, they were to let him know that they were good shepherds even though to most Egyptians, any shepherd made their skin crawl. They didn't cotton to shepherds in their land.

Pharaoh Welcomes Joseph's Family

Joseph went and told Pharaoh that his father and brothers were going to stay in Goshen. And he took five men from his brothers and gave them to Pharaoh. And when Pharaoh asked the brothers what they did for a living, they answered, "Shepherds, sir."

And they asked Pharaoh's permission to stay in Goshen and it was given.

"Have your brothers live in the finest area I have in Egypt. And if you know any of them to be really tough at what they do, then have them run my livestock."

And Joseph brought his dad to meet Pharaoh and Jacob blessed Pharaoh.

Pharaoh asked Jacob, "How old are you?"

And Jacob answered, "I'm one hundred and thirty years old. I'm not as old as my fathers, but I'm getting there." Jacob again blessed Pharaoh, and Joseph then took his father and brothers to the land of Goshen, in the land of Rameses, as Pharaoh had commanded.

Then Joseph provided his father and brothers with enough to keep 'em going for a long time.

And the famine was really bad. So bad, in fact, that money wasn't enough to get grain. So, the money that Joseph had gotten he put up in Pharaoh's bank. Soon men came to get more food, and Joseph told 'em the price was their livestock.

And after the money was gone and the livestock was used up, many still came to Joseph. "What can we do?" they asked. "We have nothing but our bodies and our land to exchange for food." So Joseph bought up all the land of Egypt for Pharaoh and he moved the people into the cities. The only land he did not buy was the land of the priests.

But Joseph did not forget the people. Even though he bought their land, he offered them a deal. He gave them seeds to plant when the famine was over with and told them they could use the land under the condition that they gave one-fifth to Pharaoh and the rest they could keep for themselves.

Jacob stayed in the land of Egypt in Goshen and they had wealth there and built up their family. And Jacob lived for seventeen years in Egypt and when it was time for him to die, he called Joseph to him. "Now that things are square between us all, please place your hand under my thigh and swear that when I die, you will not bury me in Egypt, but in the burial place of my father." And Joseph said, "I swear."

And Jacob was contented since his son swore that he would bury him in Canaan.

Jacob Blesses His Grandkids

Soon it became apparent that Jacob was sick and dying. Joseph took with him his sons Manasseh and Ephraim. Jacob was told that they were coming.

Israel set himself straight so that he might look better to Joseph and when Joseph arrived, Israel said, "The Almighty appeared to me at Luz in the land of Canaan and really laid good things on me."

And blessing Joseph he said, "Now your children are my children. Your two sons, Ephraim and Manasseh, are just like Reuben and Simeon."

And Jacob blessed Joseph's two sons, saying:

> "Before my fathers Abraham and Isaac walked, the Almighty walked. It is God who has fed me and clothed me my whole life. And the Angel of God has saved me from all evil. Bless these young men and let my name be upon them and the name of my fathers Abraham and Isaac. And let them grow into a great nation on this earth."

Now when Joseph saw that his father had put his right hand on Ephraim he was miffed. He wanted his oldest boy to get this particular blessing, but Jacob told him that he would just have to get over it.

"Look, I know that this is your firstborn, and he'll be a great person, really. But it is the younger brother who will be greater and his descendants will become a great nation someday."

And then Israel looked to his son who he had never hoped to see again in life. "I have given you one portion of my wealth above your brothers. The extra wealth came from the hand of the Amorite which I took with my sword and my bow."

The Blessing of the Twelve Tribes

Jacob called his sons together before he died. And he told them: "Come together and listen, brothers, to your father Israel.

"Reuben, you are my firstborn. My strength and the beginning of my strength. You have excellent dignity and excellent power, but you will not get ahead in life because you slept in my bed with my wife.

"Simeon and Levi are brothers. You are instruments of cruelty in your house. I don't even want to try and set you straight about this. My honor won't be a part of who you are; all because you just had to waste that man over your silly pride. A curse on your anger for it is powerful and you are cruel. Your seeds will be divided in Jacob and scattered in Israel.

"Judah, you have been praised by your brothers. You shall be strong against your enemies and your father's children shall bow down before you. You are like a lion, your prey shall fall like a lion would make a prey fall. And none of this power will be taken from you, nor can any law come between you until Shiloh comes. And I ask that you give your life to the Almighty so the people will obey. It'll be like tying a donkey's colt to the strongest vine (he can't get away). Your clothes shall be washed in dark colors like the blood of grapes, and your people will have dark eyes and white teeth.

"Zebulun, you shall be a sea merchant. Ships will come to you for protection and safety along the border of Sidon.

"Issachar is like a strong mule lying down with a burden on each side. It was good to rest and where you rested was pleasant, but now you must bow your shoulder and take on the burden. You shall become a band of slaves.

"Dan shall be a judge of his people. As one of my sons, and a member of the tribe of Israel, you will be like the serpent—dangerous. You'll be like the viper that will bite the heels of the horse, so that the rider will fall. My son, I pray for your salvation.

"Gad, it's gonna be tough, at first. Things will trample you, but you will be victorious in the end.

"Asher's wealth will be like bread and you will share this like royalty.

"Naphtali is like a deer turned loose. You will give godly words.

"Joseph is like a vine filled with fruit. Your branches run over the wall even though people have used and abused you, you kept your backbone. And your arms are also strong because you were seasoned by the Mighty Almighty. And the Almighty will guide you, bless you with blessings untold because you have it from the original source—the God of Jacob, Jacob's father and grandfather. Only God can be the head of Joseph since you were separated from your brothers.

"Benjamin is like a starving wolf. In the morning he will eat what he has captured, and at night he'll divide what he reaps."

And all these are the twelve tribes of Israel, and the above is what Jacob spoke to his sons on his deathbed. And he blessed them accordingly and each one was blessed according to Jacob's blessing.

Before he died Jacob asked his sons to bury him alongside his father in the cave which is in the field of Ephron the Hittite.

The Final Chapter

And Joseph cried and laid himself across his dead father's body. And Joseph told his servants the physicians to embalm his father. And they did. Forty days passed, for that's how long it takes after an embalming, and the Egyptians mourned him seventy days.

And when the mourning had passed, Joseph asked folks to kind of bend Pharaoh's ear. "If I've been doing right by him, I'd like permission to go and bury my father in Canaan. I promised my dad."

And Pharaoh said, "Go bury your ol' man, Joseph, as he made you promise." And Joseph buried his father. Everyone was at the funeral: servants of the Pharaoh, elders of Joseph's house, as well as the elders of Egypt.

And also with Joseph were chariots and horsemen. It was a turned out funeral. Then they came to the threshing floor of Atad, just 'round the corner from Jordan to mourn with great and solemn feelings and Joseph mourned his dad seven days.

The homeboys of Canaan saw Joseph and the others mourning and knew that it was a sad time for the Egyptians.

Israel's sons did as they were told to do by their father before he died. They took him to the land the Almighty had promised him, burying him in the land of Canaan, in the cave of the field of Machpelah. This was the same cave Abraham bought for his wife's burial. When Joseph had buried his father, he returned to Egypt with his brothers, friends, and supporters.

After their father died, Joseph's brothers thought that maybe Joseph would now diss 'em and turn 'em out. "He might get justice for what we've done to him." So they sent a scouting party to Joseph to take a message which said,

"Forgive your brothers, man. They serve the Almighty as you do." And Joseph cried.

His brothers fell down before Joseph 'cuz they were so ashamed, and told Joseph they would be his slaves, but Joseph told them, "Loosen up, and don't be afraid. Look, we're in the place of the Almighty, and 'tho you meant me no good, God did mean it for good in order to bring about this day. So, don't jock yourselves. I'm gonna take care of things with you and your kids." And then he threw his arms around them and made them feel welcome.

Joseph lived in Egypt with his father's family and was one hundred and ten years when he died. Joseph saw three generations of Ephraim's kids and the kids of Machir, the son of Manasseh, were practically brought up on Joseph's knee. And Joseph let them know that he was dying, but that the Almighty was still a part of their lives even without him. And he told them that the Almighty would still keep the promise that he made to Abraham, to Isaac, and to Jacob.

And taking a vow, Joseph told the children of Israel, "The Almighty will surely visit you and you shall take me away for burial." So Joseph died at one hundred and ten years of age and they embalmed him and buried him in a coffin in Egypt.

The end of the Book of Genesis
May the Almighty Bless the Reading of His Word!

The Second Book of Moses
called
Exodus

Go down Moses, Way down in Egypt land.
Tell Ol' Pharaoh,
  "Let my people go!"

Old Negro Spiritual

Things Just Ain't the Same!

Israel had twelve sons. Now Israel and his sons went to live in Egypt where their brother, Joseph, was a real heavy dude, even though he wasn't Egyptian. The family total was 70 or so, not including Joseph's boys and each son became the head of a tribe.

Now when Joseph died, all the families grew strong in the land of Egypt, and they were all over the place. But as times changed, there was no directory assistance on Joseph and what all he'd done for folks 'round those parts. Now there was a new kid on the block.

And this new Pharaoh, especially, looked around and noticed just how many folks of Israel were running round and he said, "Hey, these guys are living large here. They ain't even Egyptian." And he didn't want them getting too big to handle and start taking over things "cuz they might join up with our enemies and wipe us out." So he put them to work building cities for him in Pithom and Raamses.

The children of Israel were put to the test. They had more work than they knew what to do with. Still they grew large and strong and Pharaoh was perturbed even more.

So Pharaoh looked up two Hebrew midwives, Shiphrah and Puah, and ordered them to do him a favor. "Look, when you go and deliver the children for these Hebrew women, I want you to blow the boy babies away. You can let the girls live."

But the Hebrew midwives believed in the Almighty and certainly were more afraid of the Almighty than ol' Pharaoh, so they didn't do it. And the Almighty blessed them.

The children of Israel grew even stronger and Pharaoh was miffed to high heavens. He then ordered his henchmen to do as he told the midwives, so that the sons of Hebrews would be wasted. He didn't have a beef with the daughters.

The Calling of Moses

There was this brother from the house of Levi who married a sister, also from the house of Levi. Together they had a son. As mothers do, the sister protected her son for almost three months until she just couldn't hide him any longer. Taking some thick reeds and putting mud around them, she made a little boat and placed it among the reeds in the river. She told her daughter to lay low and see what would happen to her baby boy.

Soon Pharaoh's daughter came to the river to take a bath and when she saw the little boat she sent her maids to get it. She knew instantly that it was a Hebrew child who needed protection, so she didn't drop the dime on the kid, but decided to raise him as her own.

The baby's real sister said to Pharaoh's daughter, "You want me to get some Hebrew sister to nurse the kid?" And Pharaoh's daughter said, "Yeah. Do that." So that when the kid's mother came over, Pharaoh's daughter hired her to nurse him until he was bigger. And she named him Moses 'cuz it meant, "I got him out of the water."

Moses grew strong and when he was a man he saw an Egyptian beating up on a Hebrew brother. Later, when no one was looking, he killed the Egyptian brother and hid him in the sand. The next day when he saw two Hebrew brothers fighting he tried to break it up, but one of them cried out, "What? You gonna kill us, too?"

Now Moses knew that if these brothers knew, probably everyone else knew, too, that he had wasted the Egyptian brother and tried to cover it up, so he ran away to the land of Midian. And sure enough, when Pharaoh heard about what Moses had done, he wanted his behind.

In Midian there was a priest who had seven daughters. They came to draw water from the well where Moses was standing, but the shepherds there made them leave. Moses stood up for the sisters against the shepherds. He also helped them water their flock afterwards. When the sisters returned to Reuel, their father, he wanted to know how they could have gotten water so quickly.

"This Egyptian brother, Dad, squared things for us with some shepherds and then pulled up enough water for us and watered the flock. You shoulda seen him in action."

"And you just left him?" said the father. "Girl, where are your manners? Invite him up to eat or something." And with that, Moses came to live with Reuel and later married his daughter Zipporah.

Zipporah gave Moses a son. They named him Gershom, which means "stranger in a foreign land," 'cuz Moses was living with his wife in Midian.

During all this time, ol' Pharaoh died, but the children of Israel were made slaves just the same. It was a whole lot worse than before. But the Almighty hadn't forgotten them and he set about His plan to get 'em some relief.

A Real Heavy Message

Moses' gig was to care for the flock of sheep that belonged to his father-in-law. One day he went out to the desert with the flock next to a place called Horeb, the very mountain of the Almighty. And right there, in the midst of a burning bush, the Angel of the Almighty appeared to Moses. Even though there was fire, the leaves and branches didn't even seem to burn.

"Goodness," said Moses. "What's happenin' here?"

The Almighty raised His voice and called, "Moses. Moses."

"I'm here," said Moses.

And the Almighty said, "Take your shoes off, son. This is holy ground."

Moses scrambled 'round to do as he was told.

Then the Almighty said, "I am the Almighty of your father, the Almighty of Abraham, the Almighty of Isaac, and the Almighty of Jacob. I'm the one."

Moses was afraid, but the Almighty continued. "I've had my eye on the children of Israel who are in Egypt and I know how rough it's been for them. I'm gonna take them away from all that and bring them to a land flowing with milk and honey. And you, son, are gonna help me."

"You gotta be kidding," said Moses. "I ain't nobody to be doing something like that."

And the Almighty said, "I ain't sending you alone. I'll be there."

"Alright, that sounds cool. So what? Even if you're with me and all, why should the children of Israel follow me? They'll ask questions. I ain't got the answers. What'll I say when they ask who sent me?"

The Almighty said to Moses, "Just tell 'em, 'I AM WHO I AM.' Tell 'em, I AM has sent you.

"Also, tell them that the Almighty of their fathers, Abraham, Isaac and Jacob, has sent you.   I ain't changed. I'm working this only 'cuz of my promise to their fathers. Don't worry. They'll listen to you. I promise."

And the Almighty got down to business with Moses, explaining to him what he should do. He warned him that it wouldn't be easy. "The King of Egypt ain't giving up no free labor, but I'll show him things never seen before. I'll put a hurting on him he'll never forget."

But Moses was not convinced. "Look, I don't talk so well and they may still jock me 'bout Your having sent me. What then?"

So the Almighty said, "What's in your hand?"

"A rod."

"Well, throw it down." And when it was on the ground, the rod turned into a snake. Moses started to take off, but the Almighty stopped him.

"Come on, guy. Just put out your hand." The snake became a rod again.

"Believe me, man, when I tell you. They'll listen. And if that doesn't work, try this. Put your hand inside your shirt."

When Moses pulled his hand from his shirt, it was white, just like a leper. And the Almighty told him to put his hand back inside his shirt and his hand was on the one again.

"Then," said the Almighty, "if they don't believe you, take water from the river and pour it on the ground. It'll be a bloody mess."

But still Moses wasn't having it. "Look, God, I don't speak so hot. I stutter. You gotta get somebody else."

And even though Moses was making the Almighty mad, the Almighty told him that he would get his brother Aaron to speak for him. "Look, you can speak to Aaron and he'll tell Pharaoh everything you say. Okay? And don't forget the rod. It'll help you do these wonders I've talked about."

So Moses went back to his father-in-law and told him that he was going to have to go and see about his brothers down in Egypt, and Jethro said, "Go, man, in peace."

Moses took his wife and kids and put them on a donkey to head towards Egypt. And the Almighty warned Moses again that Pharaoh wasn't gonna be an easy nut to crack.

"Look, all this is gonna really make Pharaoh mad, and he ain't gonna let My people go. He'll try and get tough, but that's really alright with Me 'cuz I've got something for him."

While they were travelling, Moses' wife, Zipporah, had to circumcise their son because she really loved Moses and besides, Moses had been preoccupied with all the Almighty was putting on him. But Zipporah wanted things to be right for her sons as well, so she did a little cutting on her boy to make him on the one with the Almighty.

The Almighty sent for Aaron and told him to go and meet Moses, so that they could go and talk to the elders of Israel together. Aaron spoke for Moses all that the Almighty had told him, and the elders bowed their heads and worshipped Him.

The Almighty Ain't Playing
with You, Pharaoh

Afterwards Moses and Aaron went and told Pharaoh that it was time to let up. "The Almighty has said, 'Let My people go!'"

Pharaoh wanted to know, "Who is this God? Why should I obey Him? He ain't nobody to me so why should I listen?"

"Look," said Aaron, "let us go into the desert and make a sacrifice to the Almighty. This way nothing bad'll happen to us."

"Why should I? Look, you're taking these folks from their work. Let 'em get back to it."

Pharaoh then told the brothers who worked for him to put a hurtin' on the children of Israel. "Make it hard on 'em. They couldn't have much to do wanting to go out and sacrifice things. And by the way, don't give 'em any straw to make their bricks either."

Now the work was harder and still the children of Israel had to fill their quotas while adding the misery of gathering their own straw. Things were worse, not better. And instead of getting mad at Pharaoh who was jocking them big time, they got mad with Moses and Aaron.

"If you hadn't come here, none of this would be happenin' to us. Go away. You ain't welcome here!"

So Moses and Aaron went back to the Almighty and asked Him to help them 'cuz things did seem worse for the brothers. Much worse.

"God, look, this ain't working. Since we've come here, more work has been heaped upon the children of Israel. Pharaoh has nailed 'em."

But the Almighty answered, "Now you can watch me work!" He told Moses and Aaron, "When I'm through with Pharaoh, he'll drive the children of Israel out himself, 'cuz I am the Almighty. He'll find out I ain't to be messed with before all this is over."

And he told Moses and Aaron to go back to the children of Israel and let them know that He knew all 'bout how Pharaoh was jocking 'em. "Tell 'em," said the Almighty, "a change is gonna come."

The tribes of Israel were mighty and large.[19] And Moses was eighty years old when he came back to Egypt to work for the Almighty in setting the children of Israel free. Aaron was eighty-three.

The Plague Game!

So Pharaoh wanted to know why Moses and Aaron were sweating him. "Look, boys, why are you here? Prove to me that your Almighty is so fired up hot."

Moses told Aaron to throw down his rod. And the rod became a huge snake.

"So what?" said Pharaoh. And he had his magicians throw down their rods which also turned into snakes. But Moses' snake was much bigger and a whole lot badder. He gobbled up every last one of the magicians' snakes.

---

[19]The tribes of Israel were all a part of Moses' and Aaron's family. For more on the tribes of Israel, read Exodus, Chapter 7, verses 14 through 27.

Still Pharaoh wasn't impressed ('cuz now the Almighty had made him mad). And he said, "So what? I ain't letting them go. What you gonna do about it?"

Then Moses stretched out the rod over the river and all that water turned into blood. The fish died and the river smelled to high heaven. And no Egyptian could drink water in the whole country for seven whole days.

But Pharaoh considered himself one bad dude. He wasn't budging. So the Almighty had to send another plague.

"Man, oh man," said Moses, "you ain't got it yet. The Almighty said to let His people go. You want frogs hopping all over the place? Think seriously 'cuz everywhere you look, there they'll be."

Pharaoh wasn't buying it, though. As far as he was concerned, Moses, Aaron and their God were blowing off some steam. He wasn't budging.

So Aaron did as Moses commanded, stretched forth his hand and frogs leaped out all over the place. Pharaoh's magicians did their best to outdo Moses, but they couldn't get the frogs to cease until the Almighty said so and He wasn't saying.

So Pharaoh called for Moses. "Okay, take the frogs away and you guys can go and make a sacrifice to your Almighty."

"Alright," said Moses. "Let's make a deal. If you keep your word, the frogs will leave your houses and stay in the river. Deal?"

And Pharaoh said, "Deal!"

Moses asked the Almighty to relieve the Egyptians of the frogs, so that they stopped coming out of the river. And the people burned the frogs and everywhere you turned things really stank, but Pharaoh wasn't really ready to deal. He was getting real sore about everything the Almighty was doing.

The Almighty told Moses to tell Aaron, "Stretch out your hands so that there will be lice all over the land." And Moses did as he was told and the dust of the land turned to lice. The magicians did their best to outdo Moses, but it was no use. Lice covered up everything, man and beast.

Pharaoh still wasn't buying into it. He just wasn't 'bout letting the children of Israel go. Every time the Almighty lit him up, it just made him mad, not scared. He dug his heels in further.

Moses was told to go and tell Pharaoh that it was past time to let the children of Israel go 'cuz they had to serve the Almighty. He told ol' Pharaoh, "Let the people go, man, or you gotta deal with flies swarming all over the place. Every Egyptian crib will be full of flies." And he let Pharaoh know that whatever was done to an Egyptian, the children of Israel would be alright. "None of these plagues gonna affect my brothers, man."

And flies took over everything so that Pharaoh called on Moses to make it stop. "Okay, okay. I'll let the children of Israel go, but they can't go far."

And so another deal was struck between Pharaoh and Moses. Moses prayed to the Almighty to relieve Egypt of the flies, but when the flies were gone, Pharaoh changed his mind and didn't let them go.

Then the Almighty said, "Go back to Pharaoh and tell him that He should let My people go. And if he doesn't, a real hurtin's gonna come that will have cattle dropping dead, left and right." And it happened, just like the

Almighty say, but the cattle of the Israelites were strong and healthy.

And this just made Pharaoh madder, and he didn't let the children of Israel go.

So now, the Almighty says to Moses, "Take a handful of ashes and throw it up in the air in front of Pharaoh. And when those ashes land, boils will break out all over the people of Egypt."

Moses took the ashes from the furnace and did as the Almighty instructed so that boils and sores broke out on every man, woman, child, and beast. And this time the boils were so bad that Pharaoh's magicians couldn't do nothing 'cuz they had sores, too.

The Almighty just seemed to be making Pharaoh madder and madder, 'cuz he didn't and wouldn't let the children of Israel go.

Next day, the Almighty told Moses to get up early in the morning and go to Pharaoh once more and say, "Let 'em go, man."

"Let Pharaoh know that I have sent you and now I'm going to send something that will touch his very heart." Then the Almighty told Moses to let the children of Israel know to get their families together, and their cattle, too. "Bring 'em inside because I'm gonna send a hail so hard and strong it'll waste everything in sight."

And Moses stretched his hands toward heaven, and thunder and lightning lit up the sky. Wherever the hail struck there was fire and it wasted both man and beast as it hit the ground. It burned up the fields of the Egyptians, too. Only where the children of Israel lived, the land of Goshen, no hail fell.

Pharaoh sent for Moses and Aaron.

"I give up. You're right, we're wrong. Okay? Go to your God and ask him to quit. I'll let His people go."

Moses went out and cried up to the Almighty to end it all and He did.

And when Pharaoh saw that the hail had stopped, it just made him mad again and he wouldn't keep his deal with Moses. He didn't let the children of Israel go.

"I just keep making Pharaoh madder and madder," said the Almighty. And that was His plan 'cuz He knew Pharaoh was hardheaded. He told Moses to go to Pharaoh again and tell him, "Let My people go or I'll send locusts. If there's anything left after that hail, it'll now be eaten by the locusts."

The locusts came big time. It was so bad that the servants of Pharaoh pleaded with him. "Let 'em go. Please get 'em outta here. We can't take much more of this."

Pharaoh called for Moses. "Okay. Okay! Take your people and go. Tell your God I've sinned and I'm sorry. Alright? Just go!"

A strong wind came and blew the locusts away, but again Pharaoh was stubborn and just got mad at the Almighty all over again. Just like the last time, he didn't keep his word to let the children of Israel go.

You Ain't Seen Nothing Yet

Pharaoh warned Moses that if he saw him again, he would waste him. "I'm warning you. I don't want to see your face again, boy."

"You asked for it," said Moses to Pharaoh. "You ain't gonna see my face again."

And the Almighty told Moses, "It's time. This time when I wind up, Pharaoh is going to drive you outta here fast. 'Round midnight I will go out in Egypt and the firstborn of the land of Egypt will die, from Pharaoh who sits high and mighty, to his lowest servant."

And so that Pharaoh would know that there was a difference between his folks and the Almighty's chosen folks, not one hair on one child of an Israelite was to be touched.

"Tell him that," said the Almighty.

But Pharaoh thought he was one bad dude. He blew off Moses, telling him to tell the Almighty, "Ain't nobody goin' nowhere. So there."

A New Tradition

The children of Israel were told that from then on this month was to be a special time every year. They were told to prepare special dishes and sacrifices by killing a lamb and fixing it up right. The blood of the lamb was to be placed on the posts of the home of every Israelite on the fourteenth day so that the angel of death would pass over the home.

During this time, the children of Israel were told to eat bread with no yeast and bitter herbs cooked right into the meat. A special blessing was to be said over the food, as well. Also, every man, woman, and child was to dress in their travelling clothes, waiting, ready and able, but everyone had to stay indoors until the angel of death had passed over.

At midnight, the Almighty killed every firstborn in the land of Egypt, even the cattle got wasted. But He didn't touch one hair on one head of the Israelites just like He promised.

Pharaoh TKO'd

Pharaoh was beaten. He didn't want to admit defeat, but there was not one house in which someone wasn't dead. Every Egyptian in town wanted Pharaoh to drive the children of Israel out "'cuz we don't want no more trouble. Next it will be us who will be lying dead."

The children of Israel were finally put out just like the Almighty knew they would be. And Pharaoh was no match for the Almighty, knocked out in the tenth round.

Whatever the children of Israel wanted, the Egyptians gave them. Anything they wanted they could have, just so that they would leave.

They took their unleavened bread and kneading bowls, put them on their backs, and headed out the front door of Egypt. After four hundred and thirty years, the children of Israel left Egypt with their flocks and herds and each other.

And the Almighty told Moses and Aaron, "Can't no outsider eat the unleavened bread. Only the children of Israel when they're celebrating Passover." The Almighty warned, "No guest or servant shall eat of this bread because this celebration is all about My promise to deliver the children of Israel outta Egypt's land." The Almighty had whupped up on Pharaoh big time just like He said He would.

The Almighty then asked Moses and Aaron to make holy all the firstborn, whether man or cattle, and raise them to Him "'cuz I've made a way, brothers and sisters of Israel." Moses did as the Almighty said.

So, Passover consists of eating unleavened bread for seven days. On the seventh day there's a feast made to the Almighty. Each young brother is to be told that this celebration is done 'cuz of what the Almighty did for everybody.

"It's a sign," the Almighty told Moses, "that I brought you out of Egypt."

And the Almighty also told them to make holy every firstborn from here on out, 'cuz of what happened to the firstborn in Egypt.

Hard Heads, Soft...

Pharaoh had finally let the children of Israel go, but then his manhood had been challenged, so homedude started having second thoughts. As the children of Israel headed out into the wilderness towards the Red Sea, carrying Joseph's bones with them, Pharaoh was getting madder by the minute.

The Almighty knew that He had made Pharaoh mad again and that this boy was really pigheaded. "Moses," said the Almighty, "Pharaoh ain't learned his lesson just yet. After this, the children of Israel gonna know, once and for all, that I'm God Almighty."

And because the Almighty knew what he was talking about, Pharaoh took off after the children of Israel with his chariots and horsemen and his army. Just above camp, he saw them by the sea. Pharaoh thought it was gonna be easy pickings. He thought it was payback time.

The children of Israel looked up and saw that Pharaoh was barreling down fast and they cried out to Moses, "So we're to die out here? You couldn't leave well enough alone. It wasn't so bad slaving for the Egyptians. Better than dying."

Moses, of course, ran to the Almighty and pleaded with Him. "What's the deal? Help us," Moses begged.

"Stop whimpering," said the Almighty.   "Tell the brothers and sisters to go on towards the sea. All you gotta do is lift your hand and the sea will part.   Then the children of Israel can cross over to safety.   Those Egyptians think they're so tough. You watch. They'll call themselves getting mad and try to follow out after everybody, but it'll be the last thing they'll do in this life. Ol' Pharaoh will know once and for all just who he's been messin' with."

Moses stretched his hands out over the sea and the waters divided into two walls on either side of dry land. The children of Israel crossed to safety and when the Egyptians followed, Moses stretched out his hands again and the sea closed down on 'em, drowning every last one of them.

Making It to the Land of
Milk and Honey

The children of Israel sang songs to the Almighty in celebration of His delivering them from Pharaoh.[20] And the songs went something like this:

> "I'll sing songs to the Almighty, 'cuz He is so tough.
> He brought those bad boys down into the sea.
> The Almighty is everything to me.
> He's The Man and I will praise Him.
> He's The One and I will lift Him up
> 'Cuz He brought ol' Pharaoh down into the sea.
> The Almighty is Everything to me."

From the Red Sea, the children of Israel headed into the wilderness at Shur. And when they had come to Marah, they could not drink the water 'cuz it tasted so bad.

And because Moses talked to the Almighty about it, God showed him a tree that would help them. He had Moses throw the tree into the water and the waters were made sweet. After the waters were made sweet, Moses told them to believe in the Almighty "'cuz He always comes through for you."

After that they came to Elim where they found twelve wells of water and seventy palm trees.

The journey from Elim was long and hard, and the children of Israel spent half their time grumbling 'bout Moses. "We shoulda died in Egypt," they cried.

---

[20]The songs of Moses and the children of Israel are found in Exodus, 15th Chapter, verses 1 through 20.

"We're hungry and tired."

"Where is this land of milk and honey?"

Aaron told them that by fussing all the time they weren't really fussing at Moses, but straight at the Almighty.

The Almighty heard them, too. "Look, just before dark you'll have plenty of meat and in the morning I'll supply you with bread." So quails came in the evening, and in the morning a fine dust-like stuff was on the ground. This honey-tasting food was called manna, as it came from the Almighty. Moses explained to them that this nourishment could be eaten and told them to gather it up as they needed.

Each day there was plenty to eat for everyone, but on the sixth day they were told to gather double the amount so that they could rest on every Sunday like Moses told them they had to. "You won't find anything to eat on these days."

But hardheaded folks needed convincing so that when they went looking for food on Sunday, there was none. And the Almighty was put out even more. "How long before they start obeying?"

Hard Choices

It seemed that the more the Almighty blessed them, the more the children of Israel wanted. From the Wilderness of Sin, the children of Israel went to Rephidim, but there was no water. Grumbling, they fell back on their same old song.

"We shoulda stayed in Egypt."

"You brought us out here to die."

"We want outta here."

And Moses was beside himself. "God, what am I to do? These folks are outta control."

The Almighty told Moses to "Stand before the rock in Horeb and strike it. Water will pour out of it and the people can have something to drink."

Moses did as he was told in front of everyone, including the elders, and the name of the place was called Massah and Meribah because it meant, "Is the Almighty with us or not?"

The Battle at Rephidim

There was a leader whose name was Amalek and he picked a fight with the children of Israel. Moses ordered Joshua to pick out some of his toughest men and stand up to Amalek. He promised that the Almighty would be with them like always.

Moses stood on top of the hill where the battle was to take place. He held up the rod of the Almighty as the battle was starting full force. But after a spell, Moses would get tired and let the rod droop a little and when this happened, the children of Israel would start losing ground.

Aaron took a stone and put it under Moses so he could sit down, and he and another dude helped to keep Moses' hand high up in the air. And the children of Israel won, so Moses built an altar called "The Almighty Is My Banner."

Soon Jethro, Moses' father-in-law, heard about how the Almighty had done great things for Moses and his people, so with Zipporah, Moses' wife, and their two sons, he paid

Moses a visit. Zipporah was coming home to Moses after visiting with her father.

"Hey, Moses," said Jethro. "The Almighty sure has done great things for you guys, way over there in Egypt. He ran right over Pharaoh." He added, "Now I know that the Almighty is truly untouchable." Then Jethro took a burnt offering to the Almighty and sat with Moses, Aaron, and the elders and grabbed a bite to eat. He also scoped out how Moses always had lines of people trying to get to him.

Later when he and Moses were alone, he asked, "What is this thing you do with the people where you sit and they stand before you from morning through 'til night?"

And Moses told him that they came for counseling and to have answers to questions 'bout most everything.

"But, Moses," said Jethro. "This is not a good thing. You'll wear yourself out and then where would the people be?"

"Listen to me, man," he went on. "This ain't gonna work. Here's my advice. The people need to know, right? And they can only learn the laws and statutes if they are shown the way. Do this. Take a group of able-bodied men and teach them the ways. Then give them the job of being rulers of thousands, rulers of hundreds, rulers of fifties, and rulers of tens. They can judge the people all the time without you having to be there twenty-four/seven."

Moses thought his father-in-law's idea was pretty cool, so he took his advice. Moses chose right-on brothers and made them heads of thousands, hundreds, fifties, and tens. They made decisions regarding their brothers and sisters, but the hard cases were still brought to Moses 'cuz he really knew his stuff.

When the children of Israel came to the Sinai Desert, Moses took himself up the mountain to have a chat with the Almighty. And the Almighty told him, "You know what happened with things down in Egypt. I took the children of Israel out of Egypt on eagle's wings. Tell 'em that if they make a deal with me that they'll keep, it'll be on the one with me always. Now, you go and tell 'em."

Moses climbed down from the mountain and told the elders of the people what the Almighty had said and everyone agreed. "Yeah, that's cool. We can deal with that."

When Moses talked to the Almighty again, he told Him that everyone was on the one with what He had said.

The Almighty then told Moses that He would speak to him from a large cloud and the people would believe even more that the Almighty talked to Moses. "But don't let the folks up here on the mountain or I'll have to waste 'em. If a brother even touches the mountain, you've gotta stone him to death. Tell 'em don't sweat it, or they're outta here."

And many days later, the Almighty came down with thundering and lightning. It was a sight to behold. The Almighty spoke to Moses so that the people heard Him, and it was a truly magnificent sight. The Almighty asked the priests to come up and make themselves holy. Then he gave them commands which would help make the deal complete.

The Commandments

"I am the Almighty, your God, who brought you outta Egypt when things were tough." And then He told them:

"Don't put anyone else before Me.

"Don't make any carved objects or things that look like what is in heaven or below. And don't bow down to these things like they are anything heavy. Not ever!

You shouldn't diss the Almighty's name, using it in cuss words or rapping with one another. It ain't cool and payback's a monster.

"Remember the day of the Almighty which is the seventh day. After you've worked six days, give the seventh to the Almighty." (Remember that the Almighty made the heavens and the earth in six days. He rested on the seventh day and blessed it as right-on.)

"You shouldn't be takin' nothin' from your homeboys.

"Give honor to your mom and dad, and you'll live a long time.

"Don't waste nobody.

"Don't mess around with someone else's ol' man or ol' lady.

"Don't go 'round telling lies on your homebuddies.

"Don't want what you can't have, or what your homebuddy has. It ain't cool."

When all this was said and done, the folks were scared out of their wits. They figured it was better that the Almighty talked straight to Moses instead of them 'cuz it was just too heavy for words. So Moses went up to the smoking, thundering clouds alone.

And the Almighty told Moses, "Look, kid, tell the folks down there I don't want no gold or silver altars. Pure earth, that's Me. *Au naturel.* Nothing touching it, pure and simple."

Rules and Regulations

The Almighty believed that things would work better if there were rules to live by. So He gave them laws regarding the hired help (like if you bought a Hebrew slave, on the seventh year you had to let him go), laws concerning doing one another in, laws to control animals, laws concerning property, like breaking and entering kinds of things. There were payback laws and not following the crowd laws, and when to go to church laws.[21]

The Almighty made everyone promise that they would study and obey the laws 'cuz it was more than cool to do so. And for obeying, the Almighty promised to take care of them.

Next the Almighty asked for three feasts a year (like the Passover feast), and that the brothers and sisters make sacrifices as well. Then He told them that He would send

---

[21]Read Exodus, Chapters 21 and 22, and Chapter 23, verses 1-13.

an Angel who would instruct them on the hows and whys of the Almighty's ways.

"Obey my man and He will see to it that there's plenty of food and water, and no one will get sick 'round here."

And the Almighty sealed the deal Himself, letting the children of Israel know that He would be with them forever. Through Moses, the children of Israel sealed the deal as well. They agreed to do all that the Almighty dictated. Moses then sealed the deal holy by building an altar right at the foot of the mountain. He put twelve big stones around it to stand for each tribe, and then he made a burnt offering. Later he headed up the mountain again to have a little talk with the Almighty.

Moses was up on that mountain forty days and forty nights.

Long Nights on the Mountain

While up on the mountain, the Almighty talked to Moses about giving. "Speak to them 'bout giving Me an offering, willingly, from the heart, without reservation." All the different kinds of gifts were explained to Moses by the Almighty so that the children of Israel would make no mistakes. He also told Moses about the place of worship and how He wanted it to look, where to place the altar and what materials to use to make it. The Almighty told Moses about the care of things in the worship place, what the ministers should wear and when. He even explained how to make the garments and what colors to use. "And all this," says the Almighty, "shall be done in My name."

He then told Moses that He wanted Aaron and his sons to lead the way.[22]

More than offerings and altars, the Almighty instructed Moses to count all the children of Israel (a census), and each man was to give up a certain amount of money in order to avoid diseases and plagues, to make amends for any wrongdoings that they themselves or their children might have done.

Now throughout Moses' time up on that mountain, the Almighty continued to tell Moses what should and shouldn't be done, and He made sure that Moses understood the real deal about everything. And Moses was up there such a long time that the brothers and sisters got bored and restless. People thought that Moses was simply up there on Mount Sinai chilling with the Almighty and forgetting all about them, so they got Aaron to take their gold jewelry and stuff, and make a golden calf for them to worship, which he did even though he knew this was a real no-no. Then Aaron built an altar before the calf and the children of Israel took offerings there and had big fun.

But they forgot that the Almighty had eyes in the back of His head and paid attention to everything they did, even while rapping with Moses. And He was not pleased one bit. "Get down there with those silly folks, Moses. They've just made My blood boil."

When Moses saw what had been done, he was so mad he threw the tablet the Almighty had written on right at the brothers and sisters. "What have you done?" screamed

---

[22]Exodus, Chapters 25 through 28.

Moses at the Israelites. "I can't leave you alone for one minute. This is just too much."

And to Aaron, "How could they talk you into something like this?"

Aaron answered, "You know them, Moses. These people are hell-bent on doing what they want. How was I gonna stop 'em?"

Moses was too hot for words. First he had the golden calf ground into a powder which he made the children of Israel drink. Then he stood in front of the people and shouted, "Whoever is for the Almighty step forward and come to me." The children of Levi all moved towards Moses 'cuz they wanted to save their behinds.

"Now," says Moses to those who stood with him, "take your swords and waste everybody else." It was gruesome. At least three thousand fell that day.

The next day Moses went to make amends with the Almighty so that He might forgive the rest of the folks for what they had done.[23] Moses begged the Almighty to have mercy "on these pitiful brothers and sisters."

"Look," he said to the Almighty, "you promised to take us to the land of milk and honey, and that's cool. But seriously, if you ain't gonna be with us, even though we're a sorry bunch of folks, don't let us leave here then."

Later the Almighty told Moses it was time to "Get outta Dodge and head on up to the place I promised to the children of Israel." And the Almighty promised that the land would indeed be filled with milk and honey. But He

---

[23]See Exodus, Chapter 32 and 33, for the complete story.

also warned that the children of Israel had to really be cool with Him if they wanted things to be righteous.

Then Moses went back to talk with God and asked to see Him in his glory and all His wonderful splendor. But the Almighty knew that to look on His face was to die, so He placed His hand over Moses so that he would see the glory of Him, but not His face.

Moses was real grateful to have seen a part of the glory of the Almighty. New tablets were made up again and all the Almighty's commandments were written, so that the deal was made again. He gave the laws to Moses and Moses was to go tell the children of Israel.

When Moses came down from the mountain, his face simply glowed. In his hand he held the very words from the Almighty Himself on stone tablets, but the children of Israel were kinda scared to come near him. Even Aaron was a little scared. But Moses called to them and told them not to be afraid. He laid out the promise of the Almighty and His rules, but since his face was so bright, he had to cover it with a veil in order to talk with the brothers and sisters of Israel.

The Deal of the Century

As the children of Israel prepared to go to the land of milk and honey, they made offerings to build a church where they would worship. And they dug deep into their pockets, because it would please the Almighty.[24] And the

---

[24]Exodus, Chapters 35 through 37.

Almighty scored big with the brothers and sisters. He really cleaned up.

The Almighty told the folks to work hard six days of the week, but the seventh day belonged to Him. And what He wanted done with the seventh day was to worship Him. "Don't even light fires in the fireplace," He ordered. "This day belongs to Me!"

The children of Israel worked real hard at making things righteous for the Almighty's church, using only the best materials and most talented individuals to build it. The Almighty told 'em exactly what He wanted in it. The house of the Almighty had to have certain coverings and things to hold it together.

Brothers and sisters brought their gold, silver, and bronze. Each one of them who was willing brought blue, purple, and scarlet yarn, soul-filled linen thread and goats' hair. They dyed the rams' skin red, and used the best wood around called acacia. There was oil for light and spices for the oil which they anointed folks with. Last, but not least they used a stone called onyx for the ephod and chestpiece which the ministers wore.

For the ark and the place of mercy, for the curtains and the poles, for all the utensils, for everything that was needed in the house of the Almighty, it was all to be made out of offerings from the children of Israel. And every gift had to be a gift from the heart or the Almighty wouldn't take it.

The head of this gigantic building project was a righteous brother named Bezalel. He created some awesome stuff for the Almighty's place and the Almighty made him as well as another brother a teacher for the others.

The project was on. Brothers and sisters had poured out their hearts and their closets so that there was more than enough to build the house of the Almighty.

Now the house was this huge tent. It took the best weavers in town to put it together. Made of the toughest linen, it was embroidered with blue, purple, and scarlet. The weavers even laid a picture of a guardian angel smack dab in the middle. Drapes hung from the ceiling to the floor so that it was right-on inside the house of the Almighty. The poles that held it up were made of pure gold.

Next Bezalel made the ark. He used acacia wood and plated it with gold inside and out and all along the sides. Four gold rings were placed on the ark which gold poles were pushed through to carry it. The lid was called the "place of mercy" and two statues of angels were made and melted on the side of the lid.[25]

The place where the brothers and sisters brought their offerings was called an altar. It was also made of acacia wood and was seven and one-half feet around and four and one-half feet high. And everything for the altar was made righteous for the Almighty.[26]

Last, but not least, the brothers and sisters made gorgeous clothes for the priests. These bad threads were made of blue, purple, and scarlet and were to be used by the priests in their duties. Everything was made to be right-on with the Almighty.

---

[25]For more on the ark, read Exodus, Chapter 37.
[26]Read Exodus, Chapter 38.

And when the work was finished, the tabernacle built to perfection, the ark built, and the clothes made, the Almighty told Moses that on the first day of the month they were to set up shop. Everything was in place and the day of the meeting was on.

Then the most glorious thing happened, the toughest scene of them all. The Almighty sent a cloud over the tabernacle so that no one could enter. At night, fire raged over it so that everyone could see it. The glory of the Almighty filled every crevice of the church house which was built by His word, at His command, and for His might over Israel.

The end of the Book of Exodus.
May the Almighty Bless the Reading of His Word!

The Third Book of Moses

called

Leviticus

And now, O Lord, this man of God,
Who breaks the bread of life this morning—
Shadow him in the hallow of Thy hand.

God's Trombones
James Weldon Johnson

An Offering for Everything in the Book

The meeting house was up and running and the children of Israel seemed to be on the good foot for once, so the Almighty gave orders to Moses about what offerings to bring and how to bring them. "Tell 'em," says the Almighty, "that when one of 'em brings an offering it has to be right-on." And there were all different kinds of offerings to be brought to Aaron and his sons who were the priests, and offerings had to be just so.

The Almighty was down with everything that was to make up the offerings. There was the burnt offering which, when done right, was a righteous smell to the Almighty. There were the grain offerings and the peace offering. Also, there was a sin offering 'cuz it was the only way to be forgiven. The priests also had to take trespass offerings, and restitution offerings (the real payback) from the children of Israel.[27] All of this was truly kicking when done right and Moses was right-on with the rules so they couldn't possibly mess 'em up.

From the hand of every brother and sister to the Almighty, there was a law that went with everything that was given. Aaron and his sons had to follow these laws to the letter so that the offerings would be accepted.[28] The Almighty told Moses, "Tell Aaron and his boys that when they make an offering, they'd better do it right 'cuz it'll make Me pretty mad if it's not done proper." And Moses told Aaron that burnt offerings were to be left on the altar

---

[27]Leviticus, Chapters 1 through 6.
[28]See Leviticus, Chapters 6 through 8.

at night and the fires are to be kept going all night long. "Don't let that fire go down," he told 'em. "It's gotta stay hot." The ashes of the offering then had to be taken to a clean place, but not before Aaron and his boys changed their clothes.

The sacrifices were a holy thing. the Almighty wanted Moses to make sure that Aaron and his boys didn't mess it up, so He made the rules clear and precise.

And so it was that the offerings had to be brought by the hands of the giver to the ministers who were to get on 'em right away just as the Almighty had said. The brothers and sisters of Israel couldn't come into the house of the Almighty, so Aaron and his boys had to do it for them. But all these laws and rules were laid out to Moses when he visited the Almighty on Mount Sinai, located in the middle of the Wilderness after the children of Israel had been brought outta Egypt.

Aaron and His Sons Receive Their Calling

The Almighty took Moses aside and told him that it was time to make Aaron and his sons real ministers of the people. Moses was to take the new garments, oil, a bull for the sin offering, a basket of unleavened bread, and two rams, and then gather up all the brothers and sisters and go to the church.

No problem. It was done as the Almighty ordered. Everyone had kicked back and waited on Moses to tell 'em what they should do, which he did. And Moses laid it out for 'em, telling 'em that to do this was right-on with the Almighty.

Aaron and his sons were made ministers of the people with much celebration that day.[29] First Moses washed them with water and then he gave special clothes to Aaron with a beautiful belt to go 'round his waist. The headpiece was sweet, too. Then Aaron and his sons asked for forgiveness during this time, and they were blessed by the hand of Moses just like the Almighty told him to do.

Next Moses took oil and put some on the house of worship and everything that was in it. He also put the oil on Aaron's head 'cuz he was special and the Almighty had put some really heavy responsibilities on him. Moses then dressed up Aaron's boys in special robes as ordered by the Almighty. Last, but not least, Moses went into overtime on the burnt offerings, leaving nothing out.

Afterwards the brothers were made official ministers along with their father, and they went about the job of being priests, but first they had to stay inside the church for seven days. They weren't to leave until their time was up 'cuz Moses told them, "You leave, you die."

When their seven days were up, the brothers and their dad, Aaron, listened to the people and accepted their offerings just like they were told. First, Aaron got a bull calf for a sin offering and a ram with no defects for a burnt offering. Then Moses told Aaron, "Tell the brothers and sisters that they're to get a male goat for the sin offering; a young calf and lamb, with no defects for the burnt

---

[29]Leviticus, Chapter 8.

offering, and bring them to the church." He then told Aaron what they were to bring for the peace and grain offerings 'cuz the Almighty was coming downtown.

Aaron's sons, Nadab and Abihu, messed up real bad. Simply put, they didn't follow the rules and gave an offering that wasn't much good to the Almighty or anybody else. First the brothers put unholy fire in the place of worship and had nerve enough to lay incense on that fire for the Almighty. The Almighty then lit a fire of His own; right under their behinds.

Moses ordered Aaron's cousins, Mishael and Elzaphan, to carry Nadab and Abihu out of the tabernacle, telling them not to feel sorry for them, 'cuz they really messed up and knew better.

Then the Almighty wasted Nadab and Abihu for doing wrong, and Aaron was sad, but there was nothing he could do about it because it was the Almighty's call.

Moses also felt sorta responsible, so he gathered folks up to make sure that everyone knew the rules. He didn't want 'em having one shred of doubt. He didn't want what happened to Aaron's boys happening to anyone else. He put his arms 'round Aaron, telling him that the Almighty knew what was best and "that if you follow the Almighty, you gotta follow the rules."

The Acceptable ~ The Unacceptable

After what happened with Aaron's sons, it was important that the children of Israel have the rules laid out for them in a way they could understand. It wasn't enough that they were hip to what was right and wrong, but also those things that were rude or unacceptable; clean or unclean.

The animals which had whole hooves and chewed the cud, like the cow, were right-on to eat. But if the animal like the camel, the pig, or the hare did one or the other, that was not acceptable. The Almighty told them, "You can't even touch 'em. It is not acceptable."

There were other rules concerning birds and fish and even some insects. They could eat fish that had fins and scales, but every other water creature was off the list.

They couldn't eat the eagle or birds of prey, especially not the vulture. Everything else was alright.

It was a big no-no to eat insects except those that jumped. All the other creepy, crawly things were definitely off-limits.

The types of foods were well-known among the children of Israel because Moses was real clear about letting them know the real deal which was simply the word of the Almighty.

After childbirth a woman was considered unclean for seven days if she had a boy and two weeks if she had a girl. Baby boys were then circumcised on the eighth day. All this was commanded by Moses as ordered by the Almighty. After the unclean days were over with, there was a special ritual to follow in the way of offering.[30]

First, whether she had a boy or girl, or was simply on her period, a sister had to bring a lamb as a burnt offering, plus a young pigeon or a turtledove for a sin offering, and

---

[30]Leviticus, Chapter 12.

bring these to the minister at the front door of the church. And even if she was too poor to bring an offering, she could go to the minister, and he would make up an offering for her so that she could go to church again.

Diseases such as leprosy were hard on the body and soul. The laws of the Almighty were tougher, though. Even if a brother or sister suspected he had leprosy, he was to go to the minister or Moses and let them look at his sores. If any of the sores was really bad, it was considered a sign of leprosy and that was a tough call. But these rules protected all brothers and sisters from getting the disease from someone who might be infected. And even the priests were given special instructions on how to handle any brother or sister who had leprosy, which could infect everyone. Even the clothes of the leper had to be handled a special way to keep anyone else from getting infected.[31]

The brother or sister had to place himself away from everybody else for at least seven days. Then the minister was to look again and say whether or not he was cured. If the sore wasn't leprosy, the person just washed his clothes and things were back to normal. If the spot is leprosy, he's a leper.

Once a leper was healed, it was important that he take a day to clean himself up. The brother or sister was then brought to the minister who performed a special ceremony so that the brother was completely clean.

The ceremony made pure everything that was unpure before. The minister would go to the brother or sister and

---

[31]Leviticus, Chapter 13 and 14.

get two living birds like the ones the children of Israel could eat, and with some cedar wood, a scarlet string, and some hyssop branches, the ceremony begins.

First, one of the birds is killed, then the other is dipped in its blood. The blood is then sprinkled on the wood, string, and branches and the live bird is sprung free.

The cured brother or sister can then come out of the camp, but he can't go home for seven days. He or she got to shave all the hair from his body and wash himself and his rags, before he can call himself clean.

Afterwards, special pains are taken to clean up the brother's house so that things would be as righteous as they were before the leprosy began.

The brother or sister then takes two male lambs, one young ewe-lamb, ten quarts of finely ground flour, no more, no less, mixed with oil for an offering to the minister. The minister follows the rules laid down by the Almighty.[32] If the brother or sister was so poor that he can't afford two lambs, one had to do.[33] Only after all these things are done, can a brother or sister consider themselves clean.

A brother or sister with a discharge is really uncool. Even things that person touches are uncool as well as unclean. Anyone who touches something that belongs to an unclean person is unclean at least until the evening. Special pains had to be taken to make sure that the person with the discharge didn't go 'round touching folks or going

---

[32]See Leviticus, Chapter 14, verses 15 through 20.

[33]For more on the types of offerings, see Leviticus, Chapter 14, versus 21 through 31.

where it wasn't cool. Even the beds had to be cleaned up before things were on the one again.

The Almighty was real clear about how to go about cleaning up things when a brother or sister had a discharge of any kind. They were to take themselves outta commission until things were cool again.[34]

Making Things Right Again

Everyone knew that the Almighty had to waste Aaron's sons for what they did. It was a sad time for Aaron, but the Almighty told Moses that He desired that Aaron make amends for the sin committed in the holy place. Also the Almighty told Moses, "Tell him, don't just pick up and go into the Holy Place whenever he feels like. He needs a special invitation."

Moses came to Aaron and explained to him that he would have to dress a certain way and bring a special offering to the Almighty.[35]

Aaron was to put on his church rags and bring a baby bull with him to the church. Then he was to take a burnt offering from the brothers and sisters consisting of two male goats for a sin offering and a ram for the burnt offering. The bull was to be used as an offering for Aaron himself and to make amends for his family. He was to toss a coin to see which of the goats was to be given to the

---

[34]Leviticus, Chapter 15.
[35]Leviticus, Chapter 16.

Almighty for an offering. The other goat was to be kept kicking so that it can be sent into the desert as a scapegoat.

After Aaron did like the Almighty had said, the Almighty told Moses that he was to do this once each year for the sins that the children of Israel did and would commit. And he warned that bringing offerings to the Almighty was serious business. They were to take note of what happened to the brothers, Nadab and Abihu, 'cuz everything had to be done just right and there were to be no screw ups or else.

The rules for dealing with the blood from offerings or for eating the offerings were each just as serious as the other because the Almighty was making sure that the children of Israel knew what was expected of them. If there was understanding, there was no problem.

All About Getting Down

The Almighty was serious about what was expected of the children of Israel regarding sex. It was a bad thing to do the wild thing without a blessing from the Almighty. You had to be hitched.

And the Almighty didn't want folks peeping on people they had no business seeing naked. It was especially uncool to get down with any animals. And the Almighty was serious about this 'cuz the penalty was simple. Death!

The Almighty didn't want kissing cousins getting hitched, and brothers weren't to sleep with their mothers or any wife of your dad, whether she's your mother or not. Granddaughters, daughters and half sisters are out of the question for doing the wild thing, just as your aunt or your sister-in-law. You can't take these sisters as wives either.

When a woman was on the rag, she had to refrain from doing the wild thing and no one is to try and do the wild thing with her. She can't put her children on the altar to be burned 'cuz that'll cause the ultimate in punishment.

And the Almighty was down with His laws, giving them to Moses to give to the children of Israel.

Ain't No Business Like the Almighty's Business

Now it's important to remember that the Almighty wasn't playing 'round about how to deal with Him. "You need to be on the one with holiness," says the Almighty. And He told Moses to make sure that the children of Israel knew the score.

These commandments were serious business.[36]

You didn't go round dissing your parents. Sunday was the Almighty's day. Brothers and sisters weren't to make or worship objects as gods, and offerings were to be done correctly to be accepted.

The crops were to be brought in and given to the Almighty first. And this is with all the crops.

The Almighty told them not to steal or lie to anybody. It was especially hard on a brother or sister if he cursed someone deaf or tripped up a blind brother or sister.

The courts of law were to be just or they paid a deathly price. The Almighty didn't want a brother jocked just 'cuz he might be poor. Justice was justice and it had to be served up right.

---

[36]Leviticus, Chapter 19, verses 3 through 36.

Talking 'bout one another was a real no-no. It was just as wrong to accuse someone of a crime when they didn't do nothing to deserve it.

You weren't supposed to diss your brother, but a brother wasn't to let anyone get away with dissing someone else. Sin ain't right no matter who does it. And if you see someone doing something and don't tell, you are just as guilty.

And when someone disses you, it is surely better to forgive and forget then to go 'round plotting to get back at 'em. You really outta love your neighbor like you love yourself.

Also, mating cattle that ain't like one another can get you into some real trouble. It just ain't cool. The same goes for planting seeds: Too different kinds ain't hip. And the Almighty told 'em, "Mix matching clothes, like wool and linen, isn't just a fashion downer, it ain't happening here."

A brother who talks a slave sister into doing the wild thing puts both the brother and sister in hot water. They gotta go to court, but the sister can't be put to death 'cuz she's somebody else's property. The brother gotta bring an offering of a ram to the table, and only then is he forgiven.

And suppose a brother goes into a foreign country and plants a crop of fruit trees? The first three crops are no good, but the fourth crop belongs to the Almighty. The fifth crop belongs to the brother who sweated bullets for it.

The brothers were told to keep their beards and hair around the temple trimmed just so. A brother's do was important to the Almighty 'cuz He didn't want them looking like heathens. Cutting yourself for any reason was cause for a real behind whipping.

Don't go talking to witches or wizards. It ain't cool.

Give respect to your elders. That's real cool.

Don't go taking advantage of folks just off the boat. Treat 'em as foreign dignitaries just like you'd like to be treated in another land.

All in all, use wisdom in judging others. Be on the one with everything, including those things that measured out.

And the Almighty told Moses, "Take care to see things my way, 'cuz I am God."

Crime and Punishment

The Almighty made it clear that certain crimes would be punishable by death. There were no exceptions and when they weren't punished according to the Almighty's rule, then the person who failed to do so would die. That was serious business 'cuz the Almighty wasn't playing.[37]

If a person sacrificed a child to a false god in the house of the Almighty, it made it unfit for the Almighty's presence. Anyone who commits this crime gotta be wasted. This crime means a brother has turned to other gods and the Almighty said, "I ain't having it!"

The Almighty turned away from anyone who used witches or wizards to tell the future. "If you want to know something," said the Almighty, "all you gotta do is ask."

Cursing your mom or dad was death to the person who did the cussing. The Almighty simply blew the brother away.

---

[37]Leviticus, Chapter 20.

Doing the wild thing with another brother's woman means death to both the sister and the brother. In fact, doing the wild thing with someone other than your mate was a real dumb way to end your life. Getting busy was something special for a brother and his wife, and the crime for doing otherwise was gonna be hard for both the sister and the brother.

Reasons for crime and punishment laws were simple. The Almighty wanted a righteous people following Him.

Priests Gotta Follow the Rules Too!

And the Almighty wanted His priests to be tougher than the children of Israel. He expected more from them because they accepted the offerings of the children of Israel.[38]   The rules included everything, including marriage.

Ministers couldn't touch dead people unless they were related to them. And if they cut bald spots in their hair or in their flesh, they dissed the Almighty big time. They can't make offerings for anybody when they do this.

Also, ministers couldn't marry prostitutes or a sister from another tribe. He can't even marry a divorced sister 'cuz he's to follow the path of the Almighty. Even if a minister's daughter were to become a prostitute, it would play havoc with the minister and his duties.

A minister was to marry a virgin, from his own tribe, 'cuz the children of this marriage might become

---

[38]Leviticus, Chapters 21 and 22.

ministers, too.   And they had to be right-on with the Almighty.

And a minister with any physical defects was to stay away from giving offerings, even if he's related to Aaron.

It was righteous for those who followed the Almighty to learn the rules big time, 'cuz making the Almighty mad was a serious mistake.   There were offerings which He would accept and those He would not.[39]   For the Almighty said, "I brought you outta bondage and My laws gotta stand."

Celebration Time—Come On!

The Almighty was pretty serious about insisting on saving some time for Him.   He said, "Tell the children of Israel, these are My celebration times.   They belong to Me." So Moses set forth the days in which the people celebrated with feasts for the Almighty.[40]   These are the feasts:

The Sabbath

Every brother should work six days, but on the seventh day, the brother should give the Almighty his due.   No work is to be done on the Sabbath.

---

[39]Leviticus, Chapter 22, verses 19 through 30.
[40]The feasts of the Lord are found in Leviticus, Chapter 23.

Passover

There were special times for brothers to celebrate the Almighty's grace. He saved the children of Israel while he wasted the firstborn of the Egyptians. At twilight on the fourteenth day of the month, Passover is celebrated. Brothers should eat unleavened bread on the fifteenth.

The Feast of First Fruits[41]

When the Almighty blessed what brothers grew in the ground, He expected them to place their offerings to Him with much pomp and circumstance. The first harvest required a brother to bring the first from the ground to Him. Then Aaron accepted a lamb for an offering along with the first of everything that had grown.

The Feast of Weeks

After Passover and things were arranged for the Feasts of First Fruits, it was party time. Brothers and Sisters thanked the Almighty big time, because without Him nothing would grow.

The Feast of Trumpets—Rosh Hashanna

On the first day of the seventh month trumpets would sound calling brothers together to worship the Almighty. An offering of fire was made to Him and no work is to be done.

---

[41]Leviticus, Chapter 23, verses 9 through 14.

The Day of Atonement—Yom Kippur

After the Feast of Trumpets, the Almighty told Moses that on the tenth day the brothers and sisters of Israel were to make an offering of fire, but more than that it was to be a chill-out day. No work or a brother would risk the Almighty's anger. The Day of Atonement was a day to be forgiven.

The Feast of Tabernacles

On the fifteenth day of the seventh month, the Almighty ordered a Feast of Tabernacles where the brothers built temporary shelters to remind them of their time in the wilderness. It was also a chill-out feast since no one was to work.

Taking Care with a Little TLC

Moses was told by the Almighty to take care of things as ministers should do. Aaron was given special duties so that the place of the Almighty was given lots of tender loving care.[42]

Pure olive oil was to be used for the fire that stayed lit all the time. The lamp was to be made of pure gold and kept polished and clean. Every day, Aaron was to bring fresh oil, both in the morning and late in the evening 'cuz this fire was to stay lit from generation to generation.

Also, on Sunday, the minister was to take twelve loaves of bread and put them in two rows. Special spices and oils

---

[42]Leviticus, Chapter 24, verses 1 through 9.

were sprinkled between the rows and then Aaron and his boys chowed down on the bread just like the Almighty told them.

The Almighty also kept strict rules about saying or doing things He found offensive. There was this brother whose mother was an Israelite sister and his father an Egyptian brother. He got into a fight with another brother in the camp and a horrible argument started so that the brother cussed the other brother using the name of the Almighty.

Well, this wasn't a hip thing to do. The Almighty ordered the brother to stand trial where witnesses were brought forward to tell what they had heard. When the brother was pointed out as the one who cussed out the brother, he was ordered to be wasted for the crime.

Later the Almighty made it clear just what the rules were about using this kind of hard core language and what was to be done to anyone who crossed the Almighty in this way.

The Almighty also said that anyone who wastes another brother or sister should die. If you take an eye, you lose an eye, and the same goes for any other part of the body. You cause it to be lost, you lose it, too!

A brother who kills another brother's animal shall replace it, but if a brother kills another brother, he's gotta be wasted.

Helping Israel Fly Straight

Every seventh year the Almighty made certain days special for getting down with the Almighty. A special

Sunday church service was required by Him to celebrate with Him for all He had done.

"Look," said the Almighty to Moses while up on Mount Sinai, "you gotta get the folks to take a rest for the new land every seventh year. That means don't do nothing in the seventh year. Chill out!" And the Almighty explained that if the brothers and sisters took care of things right in the first six years, it would be a cinch to rest in the seventh.

"And," said the Almighty, "if things to eat grow, that's okay, you can eat it, but the animals are to just graze freely."

The Year of Jubilee

The fiftieth year was also started out with a special Sunday service and was called the Year of Jubilee. The year started on the Day of Atonement when folks came to ask for forgiveness. Slaves could be set free, land could be leased for fifty years until the next Jubilee, and debts were cleared.[43] It was a time for setting things right. It was a time when the poor could receive extra help, slaves would be freed, and a brother would find relief.

And the Almighty asked the brothers and sisters to celebrate all the chill-out days so that it would be right-on for a long time.

---

[43]There was a time called redemption of property. See Leviticus, Chapter 25, verses 23 through 55.

Blessings and Curses

It was important to the Almighty to know that the brothers of Israel would keep His word and do as He asked. If the brothers didn't mess up, it was right-on. For not messing up, He promised to be with them forever.

The Almighty said, "Look, Israel, if you can do this—walk in My ways, follow the rules and keep My commandments—you won't have to worry about nothing. From nobody! Not ever!"

And the Almighty pressed on, "It's really easy. Don't pray to false gods and obey my Sunday rule and it's on the one. That's just for starters."

For starters He promised that nothing could hurt them. He also promised that they would have plenty to eat. He promised that the Israelites would be His folks forever.

"But, if you can't do this, there will be Hell to pay. There is no rest for those who go against Me. Remember this."[44]

If the brothers messed up, the Almighty promised a real payback for the crime. "If you turn your back on me, you can look forward to some real heavy storms in your life. I'll turn my back on you, so that when you face those bad brothers out there in the world, they'll kick your butt! And you will be a yellow-back coward, running away when no one's there."

The Almighty told them that it would be gross to eat the kids or worship false gods 'cuz "I will wipe out those altars and blow you away." The brothers were told that they

---

[44]Leviticus, Chapter 26.

would be scattered about and the gangs and gangsters would take them as slaves, if they weren't wasted first.

Turning your back on the Almighty was bad enough, but if you didn't mend your ways, the punishment was seven times worse than it was before. And then the Almighty gave the brothers and sisters of Israel a way out when things weren't up to snuff. If you messed up, it wasn't automatic death. The Almighty was forgiving, but the offending party had to do something in return for His forgiveness.

There were ways that a person could clear things up with the Almighty. He told Moses up there on Mount Sinai just what could be done. "Look, Moses, I promised to be with these hardheaded folks and I'll keep that promise. Sometimes, though, I'll have to tear into that behind."

Payday for the Almighty

The ministers played a part in making sure that things went according to the Almighty's plans. And, of course, Moses was there to offer guidance.

The Almighty told Moses, "When brothers decide to fly right and give themselves to Me, they should make payments according to their age and whether they are a brother or sister, or even a child."

A brother over the age of twenty, but under the age of sixty had to pay fifty shekels of silver. A sister 'round that age should give thirty shekels of silver. Now a young brother should pay twenty shekels if he's over five and under twenty, and a young sister the same age should pay ten shekels of silver.

The older brothers should pay fifteen shekels of silver, but the older sisters have to pay only ten shekels of silver.

If a brother wanted to give an animal to the Almighty, they gotta stick with the deal, but just in case a brother decides to renege on the deal, he owes two animals.

And suppose a brother wants to give his crib to the Almighty, he can have it back only after he asks and the minister will give a fair price. The brother pays that plus twenty percent extra. Then and only then can he have his crib back.

Same thing goes for a brother's land. He can give part of his land to the Almighty and have it appraised for whatever it takes to make things grow on it. When he wants it back, like in the time of Jubilee, the minister puts a price on it and the brother pays that plus twenty percent extra.

The Almighty didn't have to wait for a brother to give the firstborn of his cattle to Him 'cuz that already was His. And if it belonged already to the Almighty, a brother couldn't have it back, not ever. The Almighty already owned a tenth of everything, so when a brother gave a gift, the law was clear on how to get it back later. For those things which were given to the Almighty, offerings and celebrations were a natural part of things.[45] All these things which have been told here were told to Moses by the Almighty, Himself, right there on the mountain called Mount Sinai.

The end of the Book of Leviticus.
May the Almighty Bless the Reading of His Word!

---

[45]Leviticus, Chapter 27.

The Fourth Book of Moses

called

Numbers

Oh, I want to be in that number
When the saints go marching in!

"When the Saints Go Marching In"

Take a Number

The Almighty spoke regularly with Moses out there in the Wilderness and He decided that it was time to count up all the brothers and sisters of Israel, to make a record. The Almighty told Moses, "Count up the all the brothers who are over twenty and old enough to go to war." Then he ordered that they be listed by their tribal names because of their kinship with the sons of Jacob (who was later called Israel).

From each tribe came a leader, by a vote of the people. Then Moses gave them a list of the Almighty's rules and instructions to the brothers so that they would know how to take care of things according to every man's place in that group.[46]

What's in a Name?

Aaron and Moses were Levites who were responsible for taking care of the church for the brothers and sisters of Israel. Aaron was the minister of the people and he had four sons, Nadab, Abihu, Eleazar and Ithamar who were also ministers. But Nadab and Abihu did something so bad that the Almighty had to waste them right there in the church. Despite this, Aaron and his two other sons continued being ministers to the people. And these Levite brothers were special to the Almighty, so that they took the place of the firstborn of all the other tribes.

---

[46]Numbers, Chapters 1 and 2.

After the Almighty spoke to Moses and told him that He wanted him to count up all the people of Israel, He gave Moses specific instructions on how to do this.[47] Of course, Moses followed the Almighty's instructions to the letter.

Then the Almighty gave each tribe a special location to live. Each location was 'round and about the church.

Counting Up Levis

Since the Levi brothers took the place of the firstborn of all the other tribes, the Almighty told Moses to "count 'em up, so that you'll know how many there are." And Moses started the 1-2-3-4. From the oldest down to the little babies, he counted 'em up for the Almighty.

Now Levi's descendants were divided up by groups called clans. The first two clans were Levi's grandsons. These brothers' gig was to clean up the church and take care of everything in it.

Levi's son Kohath had four clans: There were 8,600 of these brothers. These Kohath brothers took care of the ark and the tables where offerings were brought. If anything broke down 'round the ark, these brothers put it back together again.

Then there was Levi's son Merari. His two sons, Mahli and Mushi, made up the clans with at least 6,200 brothers total. These brothers took care of the frame of the church like the post and the bases for the post. They used special equipment to keep the poles up so that the church was up.

---

[47]Numbers, Chapter 3, verses 14 through 51.

Moses and Aaron (as well as his boys), kept to the east side of the church where they did their work. Their job was to see to it that everything else was done, and to make sure that the other clan brothers did their job.

And the Almighty said, "Only the Levite brothers can come into the church. Anyone dissing this rule would pay with their life."

Then the Almighty wanted Moses to count the brothers of Kohath who were among the Levites and were available to serve Him. And on down the line, according to where they were from, they were ordered into service as the Almighty saw fit.

The Kohath Brother's Gig

The Almighty told Moses to count up the brothers who were Kohath kin. "From thirty to fifty, these brothers gotta work in the church." The Almighty had a special job for these brothers and counting 'em helped to make the move easier.

As the children of Israel got closer to the land of milk and honey the Almighty had promised them, they were constantly on the move. The job of the Kohath brothers was to help carry the church after Aaron and his son had packed it up for moving.

First, Aaron and his boys were to go into the church and cover up the ark with a veil. Then they took a leather cover and put it over the veil, and a blue cloth and put it over all that.

After the ark was covered, Aaron and his boys put the poles through the carrying rings and lifted it up to be carried out. They then took a blue cloth and put it over the table where the offerings bowls were kept, which they then covered with leather and a scarlet cover on top of all that. The poles were put through the carrying rings and lifted up to be carried out.

They also had to cover up the lamps and stands and all the things that were used in the offering, including the tub of oil. Everything was covered with leather and then bundled up in a carrying case.

Then the Almighty ordered Moses and Aaron to pay close attention 'cuz He was saying this real careful. "We don't want the Kohath brothers getting into no trouble doing this gig, so make sure they got it straight when they carry this stuff to the next town." The Almighty then explained just how the holy stuff was to be carried, including who carried what to where.

And only brothers who were between the ages of thirty and fifty were right for the job 'cuz they had just the right maturity for the Almighty's taste. This wasn't a job for little boys.

Next the Almighty told Moses and Aaron to count up the Gershonite brothers. Their gig was carrying the church itself, the curtains and all the coverings. This job too was to go to mature brothers who were at least thirty, but not fifty.

Then Moses and Aaron counted the Merari brothers who ranged from thirty to fifty years of age, to carry the frames, poles and bars of the church house and all the tools.

And there were 8,580 brothers who helped to move the church house to the next town as the children of Israel got closer to the promised land. And every brother had a gig with his name on it, so that things would go smooth.

For the Crime, Do the Time

When Moses talked with the Almighty, he did his best to listen to what the Almighty was putting down 'cuz the Almighty didn't like jacking folks up for their sins. For instance, lepers were unclean and had to live outside of town away from everybody. But if they were lucky enough to get clean and they followed the law, they could come home again.

And when a brother did something he knows ain't right, it ain't at all cool. So, the Almighty put some awesome rules into effect to help a brother get through the troublesome time. A brother gotta do what a brother gotta do to square things with the Almighty 'cuz the Almighty always had a way out. Sometimes, however, the way out was death 'cuz it helped others know not to do it anymore.

The Almighty's justice was swift and fair because he wanted the brothers and sisters of Israel to do right by Him and each other. So rules were given to Moses and everything connected to that rule was told to Moses so that he could tell the brothers and sisters of Israel.[48]

Brothers and sisters were given rules on behavior with one another. And it wasn't cool to sleep with someone else's ol' lady, or to look at one another with lust. It wasn't cool and the Almighty made it clear to Moses that

---

[48]Numbers, Chapter 5 and 6

He wasn't having it. So rules were tough, but not hard to follow 'cuz they were so clear.[49] The brothers and sisters were to take their problems to the Almighty's man so that he could counsel them according to the Almighty's rules.

If a brother thinks his wife is running around on him, the brother is to take the sister to the minister. The minister then asks the sister direct, "You been jocking your ol' man?" And if the sister says, "No, I ain't been jocking my ol' man. I've been true," the minister has her hold onto a jar of bitter water. The minister then says, "Okay, if this is true, nothing bad'll happen to you. If you ain't tellin' the truth, sister, your thigh'll rot and your body'll swell up like a beached whale." And the sister says, "Let it be."

The Almighty spoke to Moses and said, "When a brother takes a breather from the rest of the folks for a while so that he can meditate and think on Me, he gotta follow certain rules." And then the Almighty laid down the law for Moses so that he could tell the brothers what was required of them.

First off, a brother who did this was called a Nazirite. The Nazirite brother had to stop getting down and partying. He couldn't drink the hard stuff or anything that made wine, like grapes and raisins. The brother's hair couldn't be cut 'cuz the Almighty wanted him to let his locks grow long. And the brother couldn't be 'round dead folks even if they happened to be related to him 'cuz it made him unclean to the Almighty. The brother had to be

---

[49]Numbers, Chapter 5.

holy, really holy, for those days were to be spent thinking on the Almighty and it wasn't cool to break the rules.

After seven days of chilling out with a brother's mind on the Almighty, the brother had to bring two turtledoves or pigeons to the minister for both a sin offering and a burnt offering. And this was a really cool thing with the Almighty 'cuz to think on Him was right-on.

Then the Almighty spoke again to Moses and said, "Tell Aaron and his boys that when he bless folks he is to say:

"The Almighty bless and keep you.
He makes His face shine down on you,
And is cool with you.
The Almighty lifts His spirit on you,
And brings you peace."

And it was done as the Almighty said.

You Can't Lead If You Can't Follow

The Almighty lay down the law for the head of each tribe of Israel. And these instructions He laid down to Moses so that he could tell the brothers who headed their family tribe. The Almighty was gonna be especially hard on the leaders 'cuz He gave them this awesome responsibility of watching over their brothers and sisters.

The Almighty ordered that the leaders had to bring their offerings to the church in six covered carts pulled by twelve ox, and then left out front. Then the Almighty told Moses to, "Take the ox and carts and use them for work 'round the church house. The Levite brothers can do the work." But he added that nothing needed to be given to the

Kohath brothers "'cuz they carry the holy things and these they carry on their shoulders."

Every day a brother from one of the tribes came and offered gifts before Moses just like the Almighty said. First there was Nahshon from Judah. He brought a silver platter and silver bowl, both worth a lot of money. And inside the bowl was grain which was given as grain offering.

And a brother from every tribe came bringing really cool gifts just like Nahshon's gifts so that the total gift offerings were twelve silver plates, twelve silver bowls, and twelve gold trays. Burnt offerings totaled twelve bulls, twelve rams, and twelve boy goats. The sin offerings totaled twelve bulls, sixty rams and boy goats, and sixty baby lambs.[50]

Throughout the entire time Moses was on the mountain, the Almighty was giving him laws left and right, but they were clear rules so that folks could be clear, too.

Inside the tabernacle were special gifts to the Almighty which were used in ceremonies conducted by Aaron or his boys. And the Almighty made it clear to Moses how Aaron was to do things so that He would be pleased.[51]

"Tell the boys," said the Almighty, "that lighting the lamps gotta be done just right so that the light looks forward." He didn't want the light casting shadows.

It's been said that the Levites were the Almighty's chosen. Aaron and Moses both were Levites, so the

---

[50]Numbers, Chapter 7.
[51]Numbers, Chapter 8, verses 1 through 4.

Almighty told Moses, "Clean 'em up in a special celebration."[52] And then He laid out how everything was to be and told 'em to get to it.

"Don't be jocking the rules," said the Almighty. "The Levite brothers gotta be different.   They gotta set the example."

And so the Almighty laid out the law for Aaron and boys in order to do their gig better. "All the Levite brothers got a job to do." The Almighty went so far as to separate the brothers from the rest of the folks 'cuz He was serious about them setting an example for the other folks. And the Almighty told Moses that after a Levite brother reached the age of twenty-five, he was to be put to work serving the Almighty.

Later the Almighty spoke with Moses and told him to help the brothers and sisters of Israel keep Passover. So, Moses told the brothers and sisters how special Passover was to the Almighty.[53] He even laid out the times and days so that there would be no mistake.

The day that the tabernacle was put up, a cloud came down. The Almighty was doing things up right for the brothers and sisters of Israel. This was so that folks could see His power and know that He was the Almighty.

In fact, the cloud helped the brothers to know just how long they were to stay in one place. If the cloud stayed a day, they spent the night. But if the cloud stayed 'round for several days, even a month, everybody knew they were to stay put.

---

[52]Numbers, Chapter 8, verses 5 through 26.
[53]Numbers, Chapter 9.

Put Your Lips Together and Blow

Now the Almighty called on Moses and told him, "Listen, I need you to have a brother make Me two trumpets outta silver to be used to call up folks when I want 'em." And when the trumpets hit those notes at the same time, brothers were to get up and come to church.

If the trumpet blew a different note, it meant to break up camp and get outta town. There was the travel sounds that meant to go 'round to one side of the church or the other. And the only brothers who could blow those high notes were ministers, Levite brothers, that the Almighty had handpicked.

Now the Almighty told Moses that the trumpets were to be used when they ganged up on the brothers in Canaan (the promised land). And He explained to Moses that blowing high on the trumpet would help them to beat up the brothers and come off looking good.

The cloud of the Almighty took off and led the brothers of Israel outta the Sinai Wilderness as the trumpet sounded and they headed towards the Paran Wilderness where they were to set up camp. First, they took everything apart like they had been ordered to, and headed out, led by the Levite brothers, whose gig it was to do this. The march started out with the tribe of Judah leading the way.

Next came the Issachar and Zebulum tribes, followed by the Levi tribes, divided into clans. And the Levi brothers carried the church and its insides just like the Almighty had ordered them to do. After the Levi brothers and the church belongings, came the other tribes in an orderly manner.

And Moses' brother-in-law, Hobab (Reuel's son), was visiting when the move began. Moses asked him to "Stay a while longer," but the brother had to get back to his friends and family back home so he said, "No, but thanks, brother."

Moses then turned his attention back to the Almighty and said, "It's on the one, Lord. Let's go!"

Grumbling Can Lead to Trouble

Despite all that the Almighty had done and was doing, the brothers and sisters of Israel still complained a lot to Moses. And this put the Israelites on the Almighty's bad side.[54] Even the manna that the Almighty sent to keep them from starving wasn't good enough. Complaining usually freaked Moses out, but this was the last straw. These brothers needed some serious talking to.

The Almighty was so put out that He sent a heavy fire to wipe out those fussin', never-got-nothing-good-to-say brothers outta the way. And folks started running to Moses begging him to get the Almighty off their backs 'cuz they knew they had done wrong.

It was hard on Moses when folks didn't believe him, and even when one thing was cleared up, another thing seemed to come back to shoot him down again.

"Why? Why me?" cried Moses. "I'm sick of these tired brothers always complaining. Lord, I need help!"

---

[54]See Exodus, Chapter 16. Also, Numbers, Chapter 11 through 12.

So to help Moses out and prove that he was indeed speaking the words of the Almighty (and also to try and get them to stop complaining all the time), the Almighty came down in a cloud so that the people might hear him speak to Moses. There was no doubt in anyone's mind after all this went down.

The Almighty told Moses, "Get me seventy brothers of the elders of Israel and bring them to the church house." And every one of them was blessed at that meeting with the Almighty, including two brothers who kinda stayed in the background, but the Almighty could see them and didn't forget them.

When these brothers bragged to everybody about how good the Almighty was, the others wanted to shut 'em up because they didn't think it was right. "Who do these brothers think they are," they complained. But Moses wasn't having it. He knew that the Almighty's hand was with these brothers and that He was pleased. He told those grumbling dudes to shut up 'cuz they didn't know what they were talking about.

Kinfolks Can Be a Pain

Moses was still having a hard time with the folks, especially every time he went up to talk with the Almighty. He kept expecting more of his brother and sister than they gave up.

Even Aaron and Miriam spoke against Moses 'cuz his wife was Ethiopian, and they turned to the folks and said, "Look, is Moses the only one the Almighty speaks to? No, I don't think so. He speaks to us, too." And the Almighty heard this.

The Almighty asked for a meeting at the door of the church. He said to Moses, Aaron and Miriam, "If anyone is called to be a prophet, I go to him directly in a vision and speak to him in a dream. But I ain't gotta do that with Moses, 'cuz he's a right-on brother. I talk to Moses face-to-face. So, tell me, Miriam and Aaron, what's up with dissing my boy, Moses?"

Aaron stood there with his mouth open, but when he turned to his sister Miriam, she was white as snow because the Almighty had made her a leper.

"Oh, my goodness," said Aaron as he turned to Moses. "Look, man, I'm sorry, really sorry. Don't let the Almighty waste our sister, man. We were crazy in the head, and didn't know what we were doing. Please have the Almighty clean her up again."

So Moses begged the Almighty to heal his sister and forgive her, but the Almighty felt that a little punishment went a long way. "Moses, if her dad had spit in her face, she'd have to live outside the group for seven days. That works for me."

And it was done as the Almighty said.

Taking a Peek

The Almighty had promised the children of Israel that they would live in a land flowing with milk and honey. This land was Canaan, which He had promised to deliver to them. And when they were close to Canaan, the Almighty told Moses to send out a leader from each tribe to see what was happenin'. This he did, sending them from the Wilderness of Paran to Canaan.[55] This way they could scope out the men there and see how strong or weak they were. Hosea had his name changed to Joshua and he led the group on the spy mission.

For more than forty days, the brothers scoped out the land in a place called the Valley of Eshcol. And they used disguises to stop anyone from knowing who they were. When they returned, they told Moses that, "Yeah, there's milk and honey, alright. There are giants, too. These guys are big, Moses."

And when the folks heard that, they refused to go any further. "What's the matter with you, Moses? We can't fight those folk. They're too big."[56] They even asked to go back to Egypt.

But Moses and Aaron pleaded with them not to do this. "Don't go mistrusting the Almighty. Not now. Not after all He's done for us. He said He'd give us a land flowing with milk and honey, and He will. Wait and see."

Joshua told the brothers and sisters, "If the Almighty is for us, then there is no problem. It's a great piece of land and if it is ours, we don't have a problem. Let's not start dissing the Almighty again."

And he was right because the Almighty was not pleased. "How long, Moses, do I have to suffer these ungrateful folks?"

---

[55]The names of those sent to spy on Canaan are in Numbers, Chapter 13, verses 4 through 15.
[56]Numbers, Chapter 14.

Moses pleaded with the Almighty, "Please. You've brought 'em this far. Don't turn your back on them now. You've got the patience to see this thing through, Lord."

"Okay, Moses. I can see it your way, but those that believe in Me will come into the land of milk and honey, and those that are plotting and scheming will have the same things done to them."[57] And true to His word, those men who caused the folks to start dissing the Lord became seriously ill and died. Those who still did not believe pretended to believe now, so when these brothers went out against the Amalekites and the Canaanites they got themselves blown away.

Making Amends

Now, the Almighty knew that not everyone meant to doubt Him. He also knew that some people had the right heart, they just were fed a line of bull which they believed to be true. So, He devised a plan that would help to rule the people who really had clean hearts, but were dumb to the truth. He also made laws to prepare the brothers and sisters for living in the new land.[58]

There were laws for giving grain and drink offerings. And if a brother didn't do it right 'cuz he had been given the wrong information, the brother had to bring an offering to the church.

---

[57]Numbers, Chapter 14, verses 26 through 38.
[58]Numbers, Chapter 15.

The Almighty wasn't gonna jock somebody too bad if they didn't mean to jock him. If a brother thought one way when it was really something else, he had to fess up, but an offering usually did the trick of making peace with the Almighty.

There were penalties for not giving Sunday to the Almighty, too. To Moses He gave the laws which would keep the folks in perfect peace.

Then the Almighty told Moses to have the folks put tassels on the end of their garments and run blue thread through it. He wanted Moses to have them do it so that "they may remember and do all that I have commanded them to do."

Sticks and Stones

There was a man named Korah who, with some friends, took to the streets against Moses.

"You think you're so tough. You ain't no better than the rest of us. What gives you the right to make yourselves higher than we are?"

And Moses answered, "Look, since you think that what we do is so easy, that anyone could do it, go ahead. You stand before the Almighty since you're so tough and see what happens. And another thing. You take upon yourself to speak for everyone. You ain't brought nobody nowhere, especially not to a land flowing with milk and honey."

The Almighty got mighty hot about what was going down. After all the work Moses and Aaron had done, how dare these men try and take over. "Moses," cried the Almighty, "tell everyone to stay away from these men, 'cuz their butts are Mine." The Almighty then wasted the wicked brothers right there in front of everybody.

But sure enough, soon the folks started freaking out. They thought that Moses and Aaron had wasted the brothers. The Almighty was really riled now. He came down in a cloud ordering, "Stand back, Moses. Enough is enough." And with that the Almighty wasted fourteen thousand hardheaded individuals in a blaze of fire. This served as a lesson to those who would dare rise up against the Almighty.

Then the Almighty told Moses to have the brothers and sisters get a rod from each brother's father's house. When it was done there should be twelve rods. Each brother was to write his name on the rod, for there was to be a rod for each tribe. And Moses told them that the rods were a sign not to go against the Almighty again, but the people were afraid.

Next the Almighty told Aaron and his sons to listen to the rules He set up for the priests and the Levite family. He gave them their legacy for being faithful. And then He proceeded to tell them about their inheritance.[59] He wanted them to know that they had found favor with Him.

Getting Ready for the Big Move

The Almighty had been cleaning house for some time. Now it was time for the brothers and sisters of Israel to clean up their act big time 'cuz it was almost time for the

---

[59]Numbers, Chapter 18.

big blessing.   And the Almighty spoke to Moses and Abraham and told them to help the brothers and sister purify themselves by making special offerings and other ceremonial kinds of things.

Then the children of Israel came to the Wilderness of Zin and stayed in a town called Kadesh where Miriam, Moses's sister, died. Moses had a lot on his mind, but the children of Israel still came to him because there was no water and started that same song and dance of complaining.

So Moses went to the Almighty, who told him that all he had to do was "Say the word, man," and water will flow. Moses took his rod and hit the rock twice and water poured out of the rock, but the Almighty was angry with Moses "cuz you dissed Me in front of the children of Israel." He had seen Moses hesitate and He knew that Moses' heart wasn't in it. So, the Almighty told Moses that he would not be able to bring the children of Israel into the land of milk and honey.

When the children of Israel came to Edom, Moses sent word that they wished to pass through. Moses promised Edom that no one would touch anything, drink any water, or bother anybody, but Edom said, "No!" In fact, Edom told Moses that if he tried to go through there would be a fight.

Israel decided for peace sake, they would not attempt to go through Edom. In the meantime, the Almighty told Moses that he was to take Aaron and his son Eleazar up to Mount Hor. There he was to take Aaron's priestly garments and put them on his son before Aaron died. And up there on that hill, Aaron died and the children of Israel were upset for about thirty days.

As Israel headed towards the promised land, the king of Arad came up against them and took a couple of the brothers prisoners.   And the people prayed to the Almighty and asked Him to waste the king and his cities, which He did.   The name of the place where the battle occurred was called Hormah, which means "utter destruction."

Yet again the folks started dissing the Almighty while they were traveling to the promised land and before a person could blink, the Almighty was up in arms.   And because the Almighty didn't take no stuff from those that grumbled even after all He had done for them, fiery serpents came down from the sky and bit the brothers and sisters of Israel.   A whole lot of folks died that day, but the Almighty was willing to forgive.   He told Moses, "Make a bronze serpent and hold it high above the people.   All who look on the serpent will live."   And those folks who were still living after the snakes bit them looked up at the bronze snake and lived.

As the brothers and sisters of Israel came closer to Canaan, the land of the Almighty's promise, they had to go through territories that belonged to other groups.   Some of these groups were hostile and jealous of the Israelites and how the Almighty came to their rescue all the time.

Through the Wilderness they travelled, first defeating King Sihon of the Amorites, then King Og of Bashan. When they moved close to Moab, King Balak was afraid that they would knock them over since he heard what had been done to the others.   He then called on Balaam, the son of Beor in the town of Pethor and begged, "Please, man.   I need help against these folks from Egypt."

"Well," said Balaam. "I ain't got a problem with it, but I gotta talk with the Almighty first."

And Balaam did, but the Almighty dared him to move against the brothers and sisters of Israel. So, Balaam sent word to Balak, "Not me, man. I ain't jocking those folks."

But Balak was persistent and begged again for Balaam to come and help him defeat the Israelites.

"Name your price, man. Anything you want is yours."

But the Almighty told Balaam, "Okay, go and see the boy. But, I'm warning you, don't bother my folks or there'll be hell to pay."

Balaam sat on his donkey to go talk with Balak, but the Almighty saw that he was a little too eager. He also saw the greed in Balaam's eyes.

Stubborn As a Mule

Now the Almighty sent an Angel to stop Balaam dead in his tracks, literally. And Balaam's donkey saw the Angel so that when Balaam urged him to go forward, well, that donkey sat right down on his behind. And Balaam bounced the donkey upside the head and told him to "move it." Well, again, that donkey looked up and saw that Angel ready to strike ol' Balaam and he nearly broke his neck trying to move away. And this just made Balaam mad. He took a stick and hit the donkey again to make him go forward.

"Get up, you lazy donkey. I'll beat you senseless," said Balaam.

Just as the donkey started forward again, he saw that Angel, and, well, he just wasn't going to jock this dude. Balaam was beside himself and took to hitting that donkey every which way. And the Almighty put words in the donkey's mouth so that the donkey asked Balaam, "Look, man, why do you keep hitting me?"

And Balaam answered the donkey saying, "You willful donkey, when I say go, I mean go."

But, surprise! All of a sudden, Balaam could see that Angel too and it was made clear now why that donkey sat on his behind.

"You oughta thank that donkey," said the Angel. "He saved your life, boy. I was sent here to stop you dead. If your donkey hadn't turned away, you'd be one dead brother."

So, Balaam repented 'cuz he was real grateful that he hadn't bitten the dust. And he went to Balak to explain to him that he just better give up trying to run over the brothers of Israel 'cuz they would certainly whip him good.

Balaam took Balak up to the top of a mountain so that he could see the brothers and sisters of Israel. "Man, I ain't touching that," he explained. Then Balaam went up and had a little talk with the Almighty and when he returned he said, "Look, King Balak of Moab. You brought me out here to curse these folks. You said, 'Put a curse on 'em' But I'm here to tell you, I can't curse what the Almighty doesn't curse. I ain't nobody compared to Him."

And even though Balak was upset about it, Balaam blessed the children of Israel and suggested to Balak that he do the same.

When Balak saw that Balaam had blessed some of the children of Israel, he asked Balaam to curse just a small portion of the brothers. And Balaam told him to "Get real, man.   I ain't touching 'em."   And Balaam blessed them again.

When Balak saw that the children of Israel would win out anyway, he offered a bull and a ram at the altar.

Balaam who had done wicked things before by using unnatural and unholy powers, gave it all up.   He wouldn't go against the Almighty for gold or silver.

And he at last prophesied that all those who went before the children of Israel would bite the dust 'cuz no one was strong enough to beat the Almighty.

Israel Getting Down with the Wrong Folks

Now in Moab, the children of Israel decided they'd take a break and party big time with the whores there.   And they even went to a couple of their idol parties to worship something other than the Almighty.

Poor Moses.   He was just outdone, but he did his duty to the Almighty and had the brothers slay the evildoers for their misconduct.   There were twenty-four thousand that died that day.

As it were, the Almighty cleaned house regularly, making sure that those who followed Him did their best to stay righteous.   So Moses was ordered to count up the children of Israel again in order to know how many were in each tribe.[60]

---

[60]Numbers, Chapter 26.

Knowing how many folks there were required that they have certain land and be guided by certain rules. The Almighty also made it clear that the laws of inheritance were in full force so that no one other than blood relations would come into possession of the new land.

This the Almighty commanded, that Moses was not to go into the promised land. But the children of Israel needed a leader since Moses wasn't going with them. And the children of Israel needed someone who was as strong in the Almighty's ways as Moses. Joshua, the son of Nun, was chosen for the role of leader, and the Almighty commanded that he be taken before Aaron's son, Eleazar the priest, to be presented to the congregation.

The Almighty also let Moses look out over Mount Abraim and see the promised land even though he could not go over.

And the Almighty told Moses how the children of Israel were to give and when. All the offerings, the Sabbath, Monthly, Feast of Weeks, Feast of Trumpets, Day of Atonement, and Feast of Tabernacles, were important to the Almighty and each was as important as the other.[61]

The Almighty also told Moses that when a man made a promise or vow to Him it was important to keep it. Likewise, it was as important to keep vows made to one another, whether in contracts, marriage, or to a husband or wife. And very few vows could be broken, but the Almighty laid these out for everyone.

---

[61]Numbers, Chapter 29.

Moses was told by the Almighty that action had to be taken against the Midianites for all that they had done. And Moses was instructed to take a thousand men from each tribe to war. They beat the Midianites, killing the men and the kings.[62]

When they returned from war, they brought captives and all the spoils of war. And Moses told the soldiers to kill everyone except the virgins and small children, and this was done.

All the spoils of war were to be divided into two groups, so that the soldiers got one half and the church the other. Part of each was to be used as an offering to the Almighty.[63]

Settling In

The tribes set up east of Jordan to choose the cities they would live in the promised land. And as they divided up the towns and cities and who would live where and with what, Moses recorded it all. And they remembered all that had happened since be brought them out of Egypt and they thanked the Almighty as they camped by the Jordan.

Later, they prepared for how they were going to take Canaan by storm with the Almighty giving instructions on how and what they should do during and after the fight.

---

[62]Numbers, Chapter 31, verse 8.
[63]Numbers, Chapter 31, verses 25 through 54.

They elected leaders to help decide who should get what in Canaan as the Almighty saw fit.[64]

The Levites, however, were to receive something from everyone as their inheritance. And this was to be done upon entering Canaan.

Then the Almighty told Moses that He wanted it made clear what the children of Israel could and could not do regarding the cities in Canaan. The Almighty also made it clear that they were to follow the rules as dictated by Him right to the last period.[65]

And the commandments and judgments of the Almighty were laid out for every Israelite, brother, sister and child. The Almighty wanted them to remember that He brought them out of bondage to a land flowing with milk and honey. It was He, the Almighty, who had the power. And it was to Him alone that they owed their loyalty.

The end of the Book of Numbers.
May the Almighty Bless the Reading of His Word!

---

[64]Numbers, Chapter 34.
[65]Numbers, Chapter 35.

The Fifth Book of Moses

called

Deuteronomy

The Children of Israel Did Dwell
for Forty Years in the Wilderness
and When They Had Fixed Themselves up Sufficiently,
They Went to the Promised Land to Rest.

Memories

The children of Israel stayed out in the Wilderness for forty years before they were allowed to go to the promised land. They had a lotta hard lessons to learn 'cuz they were often dissing the Almighty in a way that would make Him mad. Now the Almighty thought it was time He made good on His promise.

Moses was the Almighty's chosen brother who was given the task of bringing the children of Israel out of Egypt. Although Moses had their best interests at heart, they often broke his heart in two causing him and the Almighty a whole lotta pain.

Now the children of Israel were right on the threshold of the promised land which the Almighty pledged to them long before they were born. For the Almighty was the God of Abraham, Isaac and Jacob, and His hand was in everything that had anything to do with them. And even though they were willful and many times stubborn, the Almighty loved them as only a father could love a child.

Preparing for the Journey

One of the first things the Almighty did was appoint tribal leaders. There were a lot of brothers and sisters 'round and this was the best idea for keeping things together. And He expected that His leaders should be on the one with Him; but more so, they should be fair in all the things they did for the children of Israel. The Almighty warned, "I've been there for you, now be there for your brothers and sisters."

Israel's Pigheadedness

When the Israelites came out of Horeb, Moses sent spies into Canaan to scope things out. The report was great in one way 'cuz the land was right-on, but the land was filled with some really big dudes and the brothers of Israel were afraid.

So the Almighty had to rid Himself of those who were stubborn and pigheaded in order that everyone else could be blessed in Canaan.[66]

As the Israelites headed towards Canaan, just this side of Jordan, they had to pass through several small countries where the kings were not too keen on having them around. But the Almighty whipped 'em good for the Israelites, so from then on, many were afraid to come up against them.[67]

And, because the Almighty had been good to the children of Israel, Moses commanded them to be obedient. The Almighty gave Moses the laws He wanted followed and Moses passed those laws on to the brothers and sisters. Sometimes they obeyed them, but sometimes they didn't. And when they didn't, it wasn't a pleasant sight. However, when the brothers and sisters chilled out and obeyed the Almighty, it was heaven on earth.

The laws of obedience included the Ten Commandments.[68] But the greatest commandment of all was to love

---

[66]See Numbers, Chapter 13, and Deuteronomy, Chapter 2.
[67]King Sihon and Og were defeated by the Israelites. See Deuteronomy, Chapters 2 and 3. Also, see Exodus, Chapter 21.
[68]See the ten commandments, Deuteronomy, Chapter 5.

the Almighty and not disobey Him.[69] And Moses was always reminding the brothers and sisters that it was not cool to disobey Him because He had been so good to them and they shouldn't want to make Him mad.

There were blessings for anyone who were obedient, but especially to the Israelites. They were the Almighty's chosen people. And Moses kept telling the folks that they needed to remember all that the Almighty had done for them, and most of all to remember that the Almighty was their God.[70]

A Stubborn People

Over and over again, the Almighty had to put a hurting on those He loved. Not only did they doubt Him sometimes, they sometimes flat out refused to do as He said. And Moses was always going to bat for the brothers and sisters of Israel[71] because of their rebelliousness. It was downright brutal to the heartstrings.

Once when Moses caught the brothers and sisters doing the wild thing, partying and all, he became so angry that he took the holy tablets that the Almighty had written Himself and threw them down on them. And even though the Almighty brought Moses up to Him again so that He could write His Commandments down for all to see, He was displeased with Moses for what He had done. He

---

[69]Deuteronomy, Chapter 7.
[70]Deuteronomy, Chapter 8.
[71]Deuteronomy, Chapter 9.

understood, though, 'cuz the children of Israel could try your last nerve.

What It's All About

The Almighty wanted folks to be partners in all this. He didn't want them to just follow Him blindly.   They didn't have to follow in the dark 'cuz they knew what He could do. What He wanted them to do was to love Him with their complete hearts and souls.   His Commandments were to be kept and the laws and celebrations done as Moses told them to do so that everything could be on the one.   And the Almighty would take care of everything and anybody who dissed the children of Israel, in a way so they had nothing to worry about. All He asked in return was "No other gods or idols," and to be obedient. It was that simple.

For their obedience, the Almighty blessed big time. There was no other like Him.

Next the Almighty explained how He wanted them to build a place of worship. Inside the church, He had His rules and laws for the ministers as well as the people. He wanted worship to be a holy event, not just lip service. The Almighty wanted everybody to understand the rules 'cuz He'd promised Abraham many years before that those who did what he asked would be blessed. This was the inheritance given the children of Israel as the Almighty had promised.

Some Laws to Remember

There shall be no false prophets and the penalty is death. Don't believe those that claim to dream or give you signs without permission from the Almighty. It's all a line of bull! The Almighty chooses who He wishes to give dreams.[72]

You should not mourn anybody by cutting yourself or shaving your head.[73] It wasn't cool to go digging in your skin with knives and things. Tattoos were definitely out!

There were certain meats you weren't to chow down on. You can eat of anything that chews the cud and has cloven hooves. And the animals could not have one or the other (like the pig), or it was a dirty, filthy thing in your mouth.[74]

A certain amount of your fruits and vegetables was to be given to the Almighty for an offering.[75] And there were rules not only 'bout how much to give, but how to give 'em. You didn't take offerings lightly or it was like throwing them to the ground.

---

[72]Deuteronomy, Chapter 4, verse 15; Chapter 5, verses 6-8.
[73]Deuteronomy, Chapter 14, verses 1-4.
[74]Deuteronomy, Chapter 14, verses 4-21.
[75]Deuteronomy, Chapter 14, 22-19.

Every seven years all debts are canceled.[76] But
you couldn't get credit for it if you hadn't paid
on time to begin with. The Almighty didn't like
mouchers.

A certain time of every year, the Almighty
wanted folks to give generously to the poor.[77]
Scrimping on giving was not living in the eyes
of the Almighty.

And, of course, there were laws concerning
servants, for the Almighty believed in fair
treatment even to those who serve.[78]

When the Almighty put the final nail in Pharaoh's
coffin, He had to waste the firstborn of every Egyptian to
get his attention. Because of this there were laws
concerning the firstborn, including cattle.[79] The
Almighty wanted folks to dedicate their firstborn to Him
'cuz it was a remembrance of saving their firstborn's butt
when He brought 'em outta Egypt.

Celebrations

And the Almighty made sure that Moses told the people
about the different feasts and celebrations they were to
have several times during the year in honor of Him. He
was the Almighty and He had done a great thing bringing

---

[76]Deuteronomy, Chapter 15, verses 1-6.
[77]Deuteronomy, Chapter 15, verses 7-11.
[78]Deuteronomy, Chapter 15, 12-17.
[79]Deuteronomy, Chapter 15, verses 19-22.

them out of that living hell in Egypt. These celebrations were an important part of an Israelite's life.[80]

Rules for a King

And when the Almighty brings you to a land and you live there, the children of Israel were allowed to have a king over them. And the king was to govern by certain rules as the Almighty saw fit. He didn't want folks leading who were down with His program, and He certainly didn't want folks running things that weren't on the one with the rules.

Laying Down the Law

In order to be a strong nation, the Almighty knew that obedience made you stronger, not weak. He laid down the law for the ministers 'cuz He didn't want them messing over the brothers and sisters. And the Almighty took care of His boys 'cuz they had a big job of keeping the children of Israel in line.

The land that was being given to the children of Israel was filled with brothers who didn't follow the rules of the Almighty. And He was hip to that fact, so He ordered the children of Israel not to fall prey to the fast way of life.[81] You see, the Almighty knew that the fast life could be a real pull for the children of Israel, but He raised up a

---

[80]For a review of the celebrations, see Deuteronomy, Chapter 16.
[81]Deuteronomy, Chapter 18, verses 9-14.

prophet with Moses, and when Moses died, He was right there with someone they could depend on.[82] He knew that a strong prophet made a strong nation.

A Promise Is a Promise

When the Almighty promised the Israelites a land flowing with milk and honey, He delivered. He also laid down the law on how they were to keep this new crib holy. And while He commanded the people to do all that He had said, He also gave them boundaries so that there would be no property disputes. He then gave them the laws that would police them while living in Canaan.

And Moses went out to the brothers and told 'em, "Look, the Almighty has whipped butt for you and made sure that you had clothes on your back and food in your belly. And when He helped you beat these guys to a pulp, He also let you have the property, so you need to thank him. Okay?"

And the Almighty was pleased. He gave some of the land to the tribes of Reuben, Gad, and Manasseh, but told 'em, "You can't start living there until you've helped your brothers get the land over by Jordan."

There were laws that dealt with lying on another person, going to war, unsolved murders, sisters who were prisoners, inheritance, and brothers who didn't obey their parents. And the Almighty's justice was swift and strong. He always had the upper hand.[83]

---

[82]Deuteronomy, Chapter 18, verses 15-22.
[83]The laws are written in Leviticus, Numbers, and Deuteronomy. See Deuteronomy, Chapters 19 through 26

There were laws concerning punishment, and laws concerning how to treat your neighbor. There were laws concerning sex, 'cuz you didn't just do the wild thing on a whim. There were laws which dealt with who could enter the place of worship, laws concerning trashing the neighborhood, and laws between master and slave. The laws concerning divorce were detailed and included remarriage laws which the Almighty wanted the children of Israel to follow.

Disputes were handled with the law of the land, and any kind of fight or family matter was handled in the judicial system set up by the Almighty through his man, Moses.

Moving In

Now the Almighty wanted the children of Israel to have the land He promised them. A special offering was to be given by the children of Israel which would be thanksgiving for all that the Almighty had done. And the Almighty wanted the children of Israel to remember all that had been done for them, and to give the first of their fruits as an offering. Then the children of Israel were to rejoice with the Almighty, praising Him and acknowledging His greatness.[84]

Moses told the brothers and sisters, "Listen. You gotta love Him. After all, He's done this great thing for you and you can't deny it." So Moses ordered the ministers to get everybody together for a real blast of a celebration.

---

for a review of the Almighty's laws. The Almighty made it clear what they should do.

[84]Deuteronomy, Chapter 26.

Finally, the children of Israel were gonna enjoy the real deal that had been promised to them.

After this is done, as the Almighty commands, it will be official that the children of Israel are the chosen people. The promise will be fulfilled.

Curses, Don't Be Foiled Again

The people were given laws to follow. And so that they would not forget them, these commandments were put on stones for all to see and read. The stones were kept in a special place in the church, so that the laws could be carried out as the Almighty wanted.

Then Moses went to Mount Ebal and he said, "This is the land that the Almighty promised. Those who enter shall be free from wrongdoing. Tell the brothers that if they don't follow certain rules[85] they are to be cursed. But, at the same time, those that are obedient will be blessed."[86] The children of Israel knew the difference so that there would be no mistake.

And so, the deal of the century was made as the children of Israel headed into Canaan. The Almighty made the deal with the fathers of the children of Israel, and now it was all coming true. So, right there in Moab, an agreement was made that would carry them through the ages.

The Almighty did a lot of housecleaning while the children of Israel crossed through the Wilderness. So, now

---

[85]Deuteronomy, Chapter 27, verses 15 through 26.
[86]Deuteronomy, Chapter 28.

that everyone was getting ready to enter into the promised land, the Almighty returned full force.   And it was important that the children of Israel realized how much they needed to be obedient.   The Almighty didn't like no mess.

Moses' Final Days

Moses was not going over with the children of Israel to the promised land so he asked the Almighty to let him at least see it.

"I know I don't deserve to see it, but please, before I die, let me look at it."

And the Almighty took him high up a mountain and let him see it all 'cuz He knew that Moses was gonna die soon and there was still plenty to do.   Also, the Almighty let Moses see it 'cuz He really loved him and knew that Moses loved Him, too.

For one thing, the Almighty chose a new leader, Joshua. Since the Almighty was going to destroy anything in the way of the children of Israel's happiness, it was important not to interrupt the flow of things set up by Moses.

Moses brought Joshua before the brothers and sisters and told them, "The Almighty is with you always.   Be strong and don't go getting flaky on Him now that the promise has been fulfilled."   And then he told the children of Israel that they were to review the law every seven years, so that even the children born later would know how to act.

"By giving you this wonderful gift, you gotta know the Almighty loves you," said Moses. "Now don't squeeze yourselves in a corner again by not doing right."

A Thorn in an Otherwise Beautiful Rose

But the Almighty knew the score, so He pulled Moses' coattail to let him know that even though things were coming up roses, He knew that the children of Israel were gonna mess up again.[87] And the Almighty told Moses that he should write a song that would help them remember, help them hold on.[88] "Tell it like it is," said the Almighty.

So, Moses went up in the mountains for a while to write a song that would inspire the children of Israel. It said:

> "Listen up, oh heavens.
> Listen up, oh earth.
> My words come down as the rain
> And stay like the dew on the earth.
> Remember that the Almighty is the Rock
> And His way is the only way.
> Listen to the Almighty
> His way is the only way!

And the rest of the song told about how the Almighty had brought the children of Israel out of bondage. It told about how the Almighty was out there with them through the tough times in the Wilderness and would be with 'em even in the promised land. The Almighty wasted their

---

[87]Deuteronomy, Chapter 31, verses 14 through 29.
[88]Deuteronomy, Chapter 32.

enemies and made them rich men. The Almighty was in their corner, all the way.

Then the song told the children of Israel that being pigheaded and stubborn was what got them into trouble every time. It was what would get them into trouble again. But if they would listen to the Commandments and follow them, everything would be alright.

After Moses finished his song, he told the children of Israel that if they would set their hearts on Him, nothing could ever stop them.

"Don't diss the Almighty, brothers. You ain't got the strength to beat Him."

Then the Almighty told Moses to go to Mount Nebo where he was to spend his final hours so that he would finally see the promised land. "And there you will die, and the people will mourn you."

But, before Moses gave up the ghost, he gave blessings to all the tribes of Israel. Each one, separately and individually, he blessed before he died.[89]

Moses was 120 years old when it was time for him to meet his Maker, so to the brothers of Israel he said, "Look, the Almighty came to me in a burning bush and it scared me half to death, but I listened and obeyed. Each of you gotta do the same."

To each tribe, he gave a blessing:

"Reuben, may you live forever and grow large in this world."

---

[89]The blessings of the tribe of Israel are told in Deuteronomy, Chapter 33, verses 2 through 29.

"Judah, fight for your brothers. The Almighty will be with you all the way."

"Levi brothers," called Moses. "You are to teach these folks the way of the Almighty. Don't go getting wimpy or soft, 'cuz the Almighty expects a lot from you and you'll be able to deliver if you stay true."

"Benjamin, my brother, the Almighty loves you to death. Be safe always."

And to the tribe of Joseph: "You will have the best land and more money than you can spend. Joseph, your kinfolk, was a prince among brothers. Your tribe will live a long time."

The tribe of Zebulun received this blessing. "You'll be great outdoorsmen," and the tribe of Issachar, "will love their tents. Together you can't be beat."

To Gad, Moses said, "You're tougher than a lion. Anybody who helps you, brothers, will be blessed 'cuz Gad didn't mind whipping up on folks for the Almighty."

"Dan," said Moses, "you're like Gad's son, a lion's cub. You don't need to be afraid."

"Oh you brothers of Naphtali, you get all the coast of the Mediterranean as your home."

"Asher," said Moses, "may you always find favor with your brothers. You are a good friend."

And last, to all Israel, Moses cried, "May you be safe, all of you. The Almighty will stand up for you always."

And the Almighty told his new man, "Joshua, you got a lotta heart and spirit. Use the brain the Almighty gave you and you'll go far."

Moses Dies

So, Moses goes up on Mount Nebo alone. And there he looked out over the promised land with the Almighty. Then he died and the Almighty, Himself, buried Moses somewhere up there in the sky. And no one to this day knows where Moses is buried, but the Almighty.

The children of Israel were sad because Moses had been good to them and put up with a lot from them, too. But now Joshua was their leader and the spirit of the Almighty was with him. Even though Joshua was picked by the Almighty, there was no one like Moses, 'cuz he was the only one who had ever talked with Him face-to-face.

The end of the Book of Deuteronomy.
May the Almighty Bless the Reading of His Word!